D1732792

you sexy thing!

get gorgeous for beach and
bedroom **in 15 days**

amanda ursell

Thorsons

Thorsons
An Imprint of HarperCollins*Publishers*
77-85 Fulham Palace Road
Hammersmith, London W6 8JB

The Thorsons website address is: www.thorsons.com

First published by Thorsons 2000
This edition published by Thorsons 2001

1 3 5 7 9 10 8 6 4 2

A catalogue record of this book
is available from the British Library

ISBN 0 00 711499 0

Printed and bound in Great Britain by
Omnia Books Limited, Glasgow

For Nick
An Exceptionally Sexy Thing

contents

Acknowledgements ix

Introduction xi

Mind Games: 1

How *Believing* You're Slim and Sexy
Makes You Slim and Sexy

The Right Chemistry: 14

Eating the Right Foods Puts You in Control!

**On the Kitchen Table – And
Anywhere Else You Fancy:** 29

Calorie-controlled, Mouth-watering
Recipes for Your 15-day Diet Plan

Use It to Lose It: 106

Exercises to Keep You Sexy

In the Mood: 148

Aphrodisiacs

The Cut of Your Jib: 163

Tips on Clothing, Posture, Skincare and
More to Make All the Difference

A Helping Hand: 203

Weird and Wonderful Weight-loss
Products

Index 241

acknowledgements

My very big thanks go to Wanda Whiteley for running with this book and for her kindness and enthusiasm during the project. Thank you to Paul Redhead for gently nudging me along when he had every right to be much firmer and to Barbara Vesey for her wonderful editing. Thanks to Peter, Jon, Pete and Janet for their contributions, to Roz Hubely and Hattie for all your hard work and lastly a big kiss and thank you to Nick for the idea and cover design.

introduction

There is no right or wrong way to diet. Certainly, some methods are considerably less comfortable than others – for example, the effects of two weeks' worth of grapes alone would be enough to put most people off after just a few days. Some diets are also considerably safer than others. Having your jaws wired and then, as one woman knows, trying to poke through bits of toffee is a recipe for disaster.

Whichever method you choose – and let's face it there are squillions of plans out there – there is only one goal: to burn up more calories than you consume, and thereby shed fat.

This goal is not exactly new. A hundred years ago doctors would prescribe everything from appetite-suppressing herbs and drugs to blood-letting, enemas and applying electricity to help their patients get slim. Today we may prefer low-fat diets, high-protein plans or carbohydrate-cutting strategies, but we are all after the same end result: losing weight.

And yes, everyone knows what they *should* do – eat a healthy, balanced diet, exercise regularly and keep up this way of life from now until eternity.

There's just one problem with this sound-bite advice: You should have started it about six months ago, because right now there's a holiday looming, a hot date on the horizon and you're in a PANIC. Horror of horrors, you need a quick fix.

I've got to come clean: from a professional point of view no nutritionist in his or her right mind – and I'm one of them – can condone the real emergency-button starvation approach to getting in shape. The trouble is, though, that at some stage everyone knows the fear of a forthcoming strip-off, whether it's on the beach, in the bedroom or both. And this is enough to push us into taking drastic slim-down action.

The key to handling such moments is good crisis management. If you're going to do it, you must do it safely. If you need a rapid result, at least make sure you are as kind to your body as possible and avoid throwing it into a state of metabolic shock.

Happily, this is possible. There is no need to drive down your metabolic rate to the point of no return, live on liquids or exercise yourself into a state of exhaustion or injury. Trust me. You *can* get a result in 15 days. OK, so you won't emerge looking like Kate Moss, nor can I promise you men out there a transformation into Pierce Brosnan, but you can look a whole lot slimmer and firmer, and gain a stack of confidence by following the expert advice in *You Sexy Thing!*

In the first chapter I have put together some top

tips from my good friend Pete Cohen, who is an expert in helping us get our minds into gear to tackle the next two weeks and stay on track.

Then you can find out how to eat in a style that will minimize those diet-breaking hunger pangs. Foods are chemicals, and as such have profound effects on your brain biochemistry. Eat the right kinds of foods and you can help control the 'I'm hungry' and 'I'm full' centres in your brain which are responsible for starting and stopping eating. This is great, since it takes some of the responsibility away from will-power and switches it instead to brainpower.

In the chapter called 'On the Kitchen Table – And Anywhere Else You Fancy', Peter Vaughan, another friend and one of the few chefs I know who really understands how to make healthy food taste fabulous, has whipped up some fantastic low-calorie, mouth-watering lunches and dinners to keep your taste buds tickled. Peter has had his own experience of struggling with his weight and so knows first-hand what it's like to get a grip on diet and exercise and make it a priority in life. He's also about to get married, so he's an expert at wooing his girlfriend with sexy little dishes that won't lead to love handles before the big day.

And then there's Jon Bowskill, a personal trainer at, among other places, the rather exclusive Harbour Club in London. Jon has prepared our 'Use It to Lose

It' chapter. He is regularly asked to perform miracles, and more often than not surprises both himself and his clients in the transformations that are possible, even in just two weeks. 'It's surprising,' says Jon, 'sometimes I can see a real difference in beer guts and sagging bottoms. It takes commitment and dedication to the cause, but it can be done.' Precisely what we want to hear, Jon.

Finally, to complete the team there's Janet Menzies, a sort of David Copperfield in the world of make-overs, who creates optical illusions with the body part from hell. Janet has given her advice and helps put the finishing touches to the bits that we can't completely sort out in just 15 days.

In the last chapter I've looked into some of the weird and wonderful products on sale that claim to be able to give our dieting efforts a helping hand. Some may well help, many have little in the way of scientific research to prove their usefulness, but it is at least good to know what you might expect from them before parting with your hard-earned cash.

All that's left to say is Good Luck and, remember, you already are a Sexy Thing, we're simply here to make you even sexier.

Amanda Ursell can be contacted on:
amanda@ursell.com

mind games:

how *believing* you're slim and sexy
makes you **slim and sexy**

'You are' Aristotle once said, 'what you repeatedly do.' Makes sense really, doesn't it? If you go on doing things that make you feel unhappy, you will go on feeling unhappy. If you go on smoking, you will go on being a smoker. Equally, if you go on eating the foods you eat and doing little exercise, you will go on carrying around excess energy that gets stored in fat cells.

The question is, then, how do you change? How do you stop doing the things you have always done, and start doing things differently? How do you break old habits and replace them with new ones? How do you stick to this 15-day plan, and more importantly, take some of these new eating and exercise habits and continue them for life?

Pete Cohen is a remarkable man. He's a friend of mine who has written several books on the subject of change. He also runs phenomenally successful workshops around the country teaching people face-to-face how change is possible.

'You can change very quickly,' says Pete. 'If you

want to. People think they need counselling, to be taken back to their childhood to work out why they do the things they do, but in reality it just comes down to wanting to make a whole-hearted decision to do things differently from now on.'

When it comes to the subject of losing weight, Pete tells us to look closely at the word *DIET*. So why don't we take it one letter at a time?

d is for **desire**

If you truly desire the outcome of change, you will get it, Pete says. Trying or hoping to change are not convictions. How many times have you heard yourself or someone else say, 'I'm trying to give up smoking' while busily lighting up another cigarette? It is through desiring the end result enough that you can achieve your goals.

The Spice Girls knew all about the importance of desire. Remember those lyrics they belted out that soon became a teenage mantra: 'Tell you what I want, what I REALLY, REALLY want'. They knew what they wanted and they sure as hell went out to get it. They had to change their lives to get it – touring, playing endless gigs and spending hours on end holed up in recording studios, doing photo shoots and making television appearances – but their desire for success was strong enough to get them through.

How much do you really, really want to shape up for the beach and bedroom? Enough to make a change, or only enough to go droning on about it and still expecting the Slim Fairy to come down, wave a magic wand over those flabby bits and make them vanish into thin air?

When I asked Pete to explain more about desire, this is what he said: 'I often ask people who want to be slimmer what it is that they want, and they say things like:

"I want to lose weight."

"I've got to get rid of this fat."

"I'm fed up with looking like the Michelin Man."

'This doesn't tell me what they want; it tells me what they *don't* want. The only way to be permanently slimmer is to know what you want and work *with* your body, not against it.'

Pete recommends doing this little exercise to establish your desires:

Get a pen and a piece of paper and jot down what you want. Write down the first weight-loss goal that comes into your head. Don't think too deeply about this question. If you find you've written something like 'I don't want to feel like a lump of lard' or 'I want to get rid of my disgusting thighs' you will find your mind thinking of these images. So do it again.

This time write down a more positive desire. Something like, 'I want to look great when I go swimming,' 'I want to feel confident in my sexy new underwear' or 'I want my boyfriend (or husband/girlfriend/wife/lover) to gasp when they see me looking fitter, slimmer and healthier.'

Forget negative desires and start focusing on positive desires. According to Pete our brains are like heat-seeking missiles. They home in on whatever is put in front of them. Tell yourself what you want and start putting your aims and goals for a slimmer future into a positive light. The Spice Girls got what they really, really wanted, and so can you.

i is for **imagination**

Now that you know what you desire, it's time to let your mind run riot and give it the freedom and space to imagine this new you. When I was chatting with Pete and getting him to explain what he meant, he told me that we have over 50,000 thoughts a day. 'How many of your thoughts are worries or negative?' he asked me.

When I stopped to think about my thoughts, I had to admit that quite a few were negative, really. Like everyone else there are bits of my body I obsess about, even if I know I shouldn't. Since my conversation with Pete I've been trying to do it less and trying to imagine the good bits in my mind. I've also started to imagine what the bits I don't like much would actually look like if I got off my bottom a bit more and did some exercise, like actually going out for a walk every day instead of just thinking I will and then convincing myself that I have.

'Your brain confirms what you think you are,' Pete reminded me recently. 'If you keep on imagining yourself as fat you will keep on doing things to keep you this way. In fact we are all very good at this trick. It takes years to perfect the art of being overweight.

'To be overweight you have to work against nature and never really do regular and meaningful exercise. You need to respond to upsets by filling yourself up with food, and once you feel full you need to over-ride the fact that your brain is telling you that you are full and to go on eating anyway. Then, when you feel five times worse, you need to tell yourself off, get more upset, and eat a bit more. By the time you're overweight you've got a Master's Degree in managing to not exercise, overcoming natural signals of where and when not to eat and forcing food down, to stay that way.'

Scary thought isn't it? To make changes you need to fuel your desires with the imagination of how the change will make you look and feel.

Pete suggests starting off by imagining what you will be like in six months' time if you don't change. Imagine how you would feel looking in the mirror. Would you feel uncomfortable? Unhappy? Sad that you were still looking the same? Imagine the clothes you would be wearing. Would they feel good, look good? Now do the same for one year's time. Imagine looking at yourself in the mirror again. How would you feel and look? Do it again for 10 years' and 15 years' time.

Now try a different approach. Imagine how you would look if you did change your eating and lifestyle habits right now. Start really getting into this whole imagination business by picturing the new you in three dimensions. Twirl around a little. Look in the mirror. What are you wearing? Imagine how you would feel. Would you feel warm and satisfied? Happy, excited, glamorous, confident, SEXY?

Go one step further into your imagination. What might you hear? Your lover paying you a compliment or a voice in your own head shouting 'Yes, I *am* a sexy thing'?

Imagine Austin Powers getting into your brain and taking up residence. There's a character who believes in himself, imagines he is as sexy as James Bond — and always comes out on top. Literally.

Psychologists say that to fix a new image in your mind, you need to repeat it at least 20 times. We see ourselves as we think we are. Remember that you are what you repeatedly do. If you want to be slimmer, fitter and healthier, begin to ingrain these images firmly in your mind, starting now!

e is for **expectation**

'Can you imagine Prince Naseem walking into the boxing ring, eyeing up his opponent and saying to himself "Oh dear, he looks good, I hope I can beat him"?' Pete asked me. 'No,' I said. I had to admit that Prince Naseem never looks like he thinks he's going to do anything other than knock six bells out of his opponent and carry off another prize-winner's purse and heavy-looking belt.

Expectations are important in this slimming down and shaping up game. In fact they are vital to human survival. If we had not expected to be able to learn to walk, the first time we tried and fell over we'd have given up. Back in the good old days when as kids we just expected things of ourselves, life was easy. When we expected to be able to do or learn something, we went ahead and did it.

As we get older, society tries (and often succeeds) in heaving its expectations on to our shoulders and to start teaching us things like it's OK to give ourselves a hard time. It's OK to expect to be negative about ourselves and to run ourselves down.

I'm guilty of that. Are you? Do you find yourself thinking you're not good enough, not expecting good things to happen and treating yourself in a way that you wouldn't dream of treating your children, friends or family?

Children aren't naturally unkind to themselves; it's something we learn to do to ourselves in this rather odd society in which we live. When Pete and I chatted this through, he said that the trick is, next time you find yourself giving yourself a hard time, STOP IT. There is no need to expect that you are going to fail in achieving your desires and the new you that you have imagined. Instead, start learning to expect to achieve your goals.

Obviously having realistic expectations is pretty crucial. There's no way I'm ever going to look like a 20-year-old again, no matter how much exercise I do and however many sprouted beans I eat. Nor, however vivid my imagination and dreams, will I ever look like Liz Hurley. But I can look the best that my body is able to make itself given my height, the way my shoulders are built, the basic shape of my legs and the fact that, for some reason, like many women, blubber heads straight for my bottom.

It's important to think about your expectations for your body, make them real and then forget the idea of expecting that you'll fail. Always bear in mind, though, that often it's not just you who is expecting you to fail. Those around you can as well. Friends, work-mates, family and so on. Either resolve to ignore them, or tell them to STOP IT too. Even if you don't tell them out loud, do it in your head, ignore their expectations and concentrate on your new ones – the only ones that really count.

One way of doing this is that next time someone tells you you'll never change, think about what they have said, by all means, but give them back their expectation and carry on with your own. If someone tried to lend you a book about flower-arranging or fishing that you did not want you could turn them down politely, so it would remain the property of the person who had tried to give it to you. Do the same with negative expectations. Give them back. You don't want them or need them.

Start expecting that through the changes you make with your eating and exercise habits outlined here, your clothes will feel looser, you will have more energy and you will be more active. Then expect to achieve enough over the 15 days to want to keep going with these new habits. If you've made that much effort over two weeks, why expect to go back to old habits?

EXPECT GREAT EXPECTATIONS!

t is for **time**

Give yourselves time, Pete told me. 'Everyone wants everything right now.' You can imagine how *that* made me feel. Here I am writing about how to achieve a change in the way you look and feel in just 15 days, and Pete tells me that it's vital to take your time!

Actually, the two are not really at odds. OK, so we have a specific goal to achieve over the next two weeks. Yet the seeds planted during this process and the changes that come about in our desires, imaginations and expectations over this relatively short period of time can be taken on into the future to work in the long term.

'Scoffing down a whole tin of cookies does not blow the whole set of desires, images and expectations you have created,' Pete reassured me. 'When the going gets tough, keep in mind that repetition is the mother of all skills.' Going back to your new habits and repeating those, not your old ones, will set you back on track.

Give yourself time for the big picture to develop, but also give yourself time on a day-to-day basis. Time to shop for foods that will help you become slimmer, fitter and healthier. Time to write a list so that there is more chance of sticking to it. Time to shop when you aren't feeling hungry or vulnerable and likely to go mad in the supermarket stocking up with things that won't nourish your body in the way you really want to.

Also give yourself time to eat, for heaven's sake. Pete reminded me that we should give our bodies time to register that they have been given some food and to allow natural systems to kick in and let us know when we've had enough. 'Our stomachs contain sensory nerves that can communicate very

effectively with our brains, if they're given a chance. They tell us when we're hungry and thirsty and when we're satisfied.

'Overweight people have learned how to override this system and to just keep on eating. In order to lose weight we need to look out for these signals and listen to our stomachs so that we can start cooperating with our own bodies again. Eating's important enough to give it your full attention. After all, you wouldn't watch television while you were making love – would you?' Well, let's hope not.

Try slowing down when you eat. How can you enjoy every mouthful if you go at it like a steam train? Put your knife and fork down between bites and think about how it tastes and feels in your mouth. Enjoy it. Get the most out of it. Put the pleasure back into eating.

Time is also an important factor in dealing with cravings. They are, says Pete, like waves. 'Don't be wiped out by the urge to eat when you're not hungry. Ride the urge, like surfing a wave. Do something else and the craving to eat will go away.'

Also, consider this. Often the idea that you want to eat is actually no more than your body's need for water. Dehydration and hunger can easily be confused. If you think a pang of hunger has just hit, drink some water instead of eating. It's amazing how often this is at the root of the thing you thought was your tummy wanting food.

Of course you also need to put practical amounts of time aside to complete the exercise program. I've tried Jon Bowskill's daily routine and I think that realistically you need to devote an hour to complete each day's plan. Make the time when it most suits you. This may be in the morning, during the day or at night. It may be that you will need to be flexible. Whenever you do it, make time for it. It is going to be one of your priorities over the next two weeks and, hopefully, once you see how great it makes you look and feel, will spur you on to devote time to exercise for life.

Pete's passing shot on time is to slow down, give your new life patterns a chance and don't say, 'I haven't got time'. MAKE time.

summing **up**

The power of the mind in achieving your goals is immeasurable. Lots of famous people knew that. Take the French author Réné Descartes. He said 'I think, therefore I am.' How about Winston Churchill: 'Never give in. Never, never, never, never' was his war cry. William Chrysler said, 'The real secret of success is enthusiasm,' and Albert Einstein told us that 'Imagination is more important than knowledge.'

To help you follow the *You Sexy Thing!* 15-day eating and exercise plan, work out what you desire

from it. Imagine how you will look at the end of it. Expect that you are going to achieve it, and give yourself space and time to do it.

the right chemistry:

eating the right foods puts you in
control

Diets are no picnic. Giving up your usual eating habits and taking up more calorie-burning activities takes effort. That's pretty obvious really, isn't it? If it weren't a bit of a pain, none of us would be in the situation we now find ourselves: needing to shed some flab *pronto*.

That said, there are ways of approaching the food bit of the equation that can make dieting a whole lot more palatable. Just as good relationships require the right chemistry to function smoothly, so too does your body to maintain equilibrium. The kinds of foods and times at which you eat them can profoundly affect blood and brain chemistry, with certain types and combinations seemingly capable of reducing hunger pangs and helping to switch off the 'I'm hungry' signals and the body's tendency to lay down fat.

Being able to do this allows brainpower to take over from will-power. Genuinely not wanting to pig out on, whatever your main weakness, happens to be a much easier way of avoiding it than relying on sheer will-power alone.

switching off **hunger**

Hunger is not something we should hate. It is, after all, a rather essential survival tool; it's just that these days most of us in Western cultures don't really use it as a mechanism telling us that we should eat. Food is everywhere, it is accessible, tasty, tempting and advertised and promoted to the nth degree.

In the days when food was less abundant and organizing supper meant sending the men-folk off on a hunt while the women scrabbled around collecting berries, nuts and anything else that looked vaguely edible, hunger came in handy. It made the men hunt harder and the women search for longer.

In evolutionary terms it's been a very short hop since these times, and our bodies haven't had time to readjust to the contemporary abundance. Controlling hunger to avoid over-eating is the challenge we face, unlike our ancestors who used their hunger in the daily drive for survival.

Scientists looking into the whole area of hunger have revealed some interesting insights that may prove helpful to the would-be dieter. While the business of hunger is enormously complex and no researcher even pretends to have unravelled it, science has at least been able to identify that hunger is dealt with by a part of the brain called the hypothalamus. It receives and processes information from all around the body, including the stomach, the level of nutrients in the blood, smells detected by the nose, tastes from the taste buds and visual stimulation transmitted from the eyes.

It's easy to put your hypothalamus to the test and to prove to yourself how powerful its signals can be. Imagine a food that turns your stomach. Maybe something you were force-fed as a child, something you ate that gave you food poisoning and made you sick, something that just the smell of makes you grimace at the thought of having to eat.

Signals are coming from your brain that are putting you off the idea of eating. The thoughts are dulling your hunger. If that food were put in front of you right now, it would kill your hunger stone dead, even if you were really in need of some food.

Now think of something you love digging into. A big bowl of ice cream, a pile of hot buttered toast, a plate of cake. Suddenly that hunger centre is twitching, saliva starts flowing and you could down any of these treats in one.

There are some scientists who believe that, similarly, certain foods are able to help switch on and off the hunger signals which in turn make you want to (or not want to) eat.

the importance of protein
Some researchers propose, for example, that foods rich in protein are the best ones to switch off hunger

signals and thus help you to stop eating naturally. Protein foods are the ones found in the table below. It seems that because the body has almost no capacity to store protein, the brain quickly detects when it has had enough and sends signals to tell you to stop eating any more.

Consider this. Imagine sitting down to a dinner of steak or chicken with no accompaniments. After eating one serving, it is unlikely that you would be tempted if someone offered you another portion. The same probably could not be said of chocolate gateaux, of which after one helping you could probably easily find room for another. The desire to keep eating such a treat is really not diminished after one serving, often instead having the opposite effect of making you want more.

By including a good amount of protein in meals and snacks and by eating the protein part of the meal first, it is thought that we can help our brains detect when we have had enough, allowing them to send 'I'm full' signals out and thus get us to stop eating.

foods rich in protein

All of the meat, poultry and game in this list should be extra lean and served trimmed of fat and without skin.

- beef
- pork
- lamb

- **ham**
- **chicken**
- **turkey**
- **game**
- **duck**
- **eggs**
- **milk**
- **tofu (bean curd)**
- **textured vegetable protein**
- **quorn products**
- **pulses**

how fat wrecks this process

This is all well and good, however meals are made up of a variety of foods, not just protein-rich ones. When it comes to fatty foods our brains seem to have a complete aberration. It appears from research that, unlike with protein, our brains are pretty hopeless at recognizing when we have had enough fat. It is thought this may be because our bodies have an endless capacity to store it for rainy days and lean times. This might have been a useful survival mechanism thousands and thousands of years ago when food was thin on the ground, especially during winter months, but frankly, in this new millennium, we're as likely to welcome such a phenomenon as turkeys welcome Christmas.

If the brain can't tell us when to stop eating fat, then it's up to us to give it a helping hand.

Apparently it's a bit of a Catch-22 situation, where we have to consciously take the first step. The more fat we eat, the more we crave it and conversely, the less we eat, the less we want it. This is said to be down, in part, to a hormone called galanin that whizzes around the brain.

The more fatty foods we eat, the more galanin we make. The more galanin we make, the more we crave fat. On the other hand, the less fat we eat the lower our galanin levels and the less we crave it.

Sadly, of course, re-training our brains this way involves a bit of a withdrawal period as we reduce our galanin, but spookily it does seem to work. I've tried it and frankly, from being a big fried potatoes fiend, if someone puts them in front of me now they seem incredibly rich. Not only that, I don't feel that dreadful battle in my head where I say 'No, you shouldn't,' yet find my hand just taking over and almost force-feeding me. Genuinely not wanting them by letting your brain take away the strain is truly liberating.

foods rich in fat

- butter
- margarine
- oils
- cream
- cheeses
- sausages

- **burgers**
- **pies**
- **chips/french fries**
- **crisps/potato chips**
- **ready meals**
- **cakes**
- **biscuits/cookies**
- **chocolate**

One of the good reasons for getting fat intakes under control is that it means the calorie density of your diet tends to go down automatically. Fats supply twice the calories of protein-rich foods and twice the amount found in carbohydrate foods like bread, pasta and potatoes.

It also means that the fats you do eat can come from sources that are useful to the body because they supply essential fatty acids (EFAs). EFAs are found in oily fish like salmon and mackerel, in seeds and nuts and plant oils. It is crucial that we get some of these in our diets. They help keep insulin, a hormone involved in fat storage which we'll talk about in just a moment, working properly. Not only that, they help to keep the brain healthy, the skin in good condition and blood flowing freely, which reduces the risk of blocked arteries and thus heart disease and possibly also impotence.

foods supplying essential fats

- oily fish like mackerel, sardines, salmon, tuna and herrings
- nuts
- seeds
- flaxseed oil
- evening primrose and fish oils

carbo cravings

With all the talk of very low-fat diets over the last 10 years, there has been a tendency to think 'Great, I'll pig out on carbs.' Sadly this isn't the answer for losing weight. Sure, carbohydrate-rich foods such as bread, potatoes, rice and pasta have half the calories gram for gram of fatty foods. That's marvellous. Well, it's marvellous if you don't get it into your head that this is a licence to gorge on them.

Eating excessive amounts of carbs means gaining weight, as you've probably discovered. The sad fact is we can't create or destroy energy or calories. They just keep circulating in this big old world of ours, and if you eat more than you need – whether it's protein, fat or carbohydrates – the end result is an increase in weight.

Although carbohydrate-rich foods do tend to switch off hunger centres more effectively than fatty foods, it is quite easy to go on munching them, especially the more appetizing ones that get broken down rapidly by the digestive system and lead to instant sugar highs in the bloodstream. Eating lots of these carbohydrates can turn your body into a fat-storing machine.

insulin – the great fat storer

The reason why certain quick-releasing carbohydrates are said to lead to increased fat storage seems to be down to the hormone insulin. Insulin is vital to our existence because it keeps levels of sugar in our blood constant.

When levels of blood sugar rise after eating, insulin rushes into the blood to take excess sugar away, thus rapidly bringing levels back to normal. The more quickly digested the carbohydrate eaten, the more insulin is released to deal with it.

As well as keeping blood sugar levels steady, insulin also plays a vital role in determining when and how we store fat. The more insulin that is around in response to quick-releasing carbohydrates, the more likely it seems that this insulin will turn the excess calories into fat and dump this in your fat cells.

Another good reason for keeping insulin levels down is that when its levels are high you appear to crave more carbohydrates. Another dietary Catch-22.

The key to keeping insulin levels down is to eat the types of carbohydrates that do not get broken down quickly but take a while before they gently trickle into the bloodstream.

To make things easy, scientists have tested lots of different carbohydrate foods to discover how they effect insulin release and have then given them a number. They call it the glycaemic index or GI number, which can be between 1 and 100. Those that lead to low levels of insulin release have a GI number of less than 55. These are the good guys and the ones we should be eating.

Foods with a figure of between 55 and 70 are considered to be medium GI foods, stimulating a medium amount of insulin. These should be eaten in moderation.

Foods with a GI number above 70 raise blood sugar and insulin levels rapidly, and need to be kept to a minimum when following our 15-day plan.

low GI foods

- muesli
- porridge
- sultana (raisin) bran cereal
- *Special K* cereal
- buckwheat
- bulgur
- pasta
- mixed grain breads
- rye bread
- baked beans
- butter beans
- chick peas

- haricot beans
- kidney beans
- lentils
- soya beans
- peas
- sweet potatoes
- green leafy vegetables
- carrots
- apples
- apricots
- bananas
- cherries
- grapefruit
- grapes
- kiwifruit
- oranges
- peaches
- pears
- plums
- skimmed milk
- yoghurt
- lentil soup
- tomato soup

medium GI foods

- puffed wheat cereal
- basmati rice
- taco shells
- bagels

- croissants
- crumpets
- pitta bread
- white bread
- ryvita (crispbreads)
- oatmeal biscuits/cookies
- fat-free popcorn
- beetroot
- new potatoes
- sweet corn
- yams
- mangoes
- pawpaw
- pineapple
- raisins
- sultanas
- orange juice
- honey
- sugar

high GI foods

- sugar-coated cereals
- chocolate-coated cereals
- rice
- sweet biscuits
- sweet drinks
- jelly beans
- glucose

so what *can* i **eat?!**

Good question. It's sometimes hard to work out what you should actually be eating. The bottom line is that all meals and snacks should help to feed your brain to switch off hunger, and should contain the kinds of things that will keep blood sugar (and thus insulin levels) stable.

This means that in practice you need some protein and some slow-release carbohydrate at each meal, and that snacks should either be a combination of these or contain one or the other.

Fatty foods need to be pared right down, leaving room for those that supply plenty of essential fats.

Peter Vaughan and I have worked hard to take all of this and turn the theory into meals that taste divine. Turn to page 32 for a good flick through the treats you have in store. For people who haven't got the time or can't be bothered to cook, I've given you a no-cook version that tries to apply the same principles, so there's really no excuse. Not only that, I've supplied the best options if you go out to fast food places, get faced with a lunchtime crisis and are up the creek without a piece of rye bread, or are simply in need of a snack RIGHT NOW.

fast food **choices**

burger places

Go for the plainest burger around minus the fries.
Have it with a carton of milk or some orange juice.

fried chicken places

Stick with a small piece of fried chicken and fill up
on baked beans and corn on the cob (without smoth-
ering it in butter). Skip the fries.

kebab house

Have one or two shish kebabs if necessary, and avoid
the 'Doner' or 'Gyro' versions and the side orders
like the plague.

indian take-aways

Tandoori chicken is a good bet. Forget any of the
curries with creamy sauces. Plain Basmati rice, not
fried rice, should be your choice.

chinese

Renowned for following a naturally healthy diet, the
Chinese menu still poses some pitfalls. Good
options would be stir-fried chicken, pork or vegetables, and some plain boiled (not fried!) rice.

jacket potatoes

Have a baked potato without butter and fill with baked beans, chilli or sweetcorn. Avoid mayonnaise-coated tuna or prawns and forget about the great mounds of cheese.

Now on to the recipes for your individual 15-day diet plan!

on the kitchen table – and anywhere else you fancy:

calorie-controlled, mouth-watering
recipes for your **15-day diet plan**

Right, now you've read the theory, it's time to put things into practice. The *You Sexy Thing!* 15-day diet plan is pretty straightforward and easy to follow. The basic rules go like this:

breakfasts provide 300 calories each
lunches provide 400 calories each
dinners provide 400 calories each

This means that in total for breakfast, lunch and dinner you will consume 1,100 calories a day. Add to this 100 calories for half a pint of skimmed milk and this brings the total for the day to 1,200 calories.

This is the basic plan. Most, however, will need to eat more than this and can add to the day's total through having extra calories in the form of the listed 100- and 50-calorie extras we'll call 'Love Bites'.

To work out the right calories for you – given that we are aiming not for some miraculous 'lose 10 pounds in 10 days' scheme in which most of the loss is water, muscle and bone, but a more sensible 2 pounds of fat a week – you need to calculate how many calories you currently must be eating in order to maintain your current weight.

You can do this quite accurately by using the equation on pages 114 and 115. The figure you come up with might surprise you, but consider this: the average 16-stone (224-pound/102-kg) woman can easily burn up 2,600–2,800 calories a day.

Once you have your own calorie figure worked out, you need to take off 700 calories a day to get to the total number you should be allowing yourself every day. Another 300 calories at least will be burned up with Jon's exercises, so you will be at the very minimum a good 1,000 calories down on your normal intake. This will lead to a steady 2-pound loss of fat per week and not slow your metabolism down.

If this seems too complicated, then you can make a rough estimate of your calorie needs as follows:

Women with more than 3 stone (42 lb/19 kg) to lose to get down to their normal body weight should plan to eat at least 1,600 calories a day. Men with this much to lose should stick to 1,800.

Women with less than 3 stone to lose to get down to their normal body weight should plan to eat at least 1,400 calories a day. Men with this much to lose should stick to 1,600.

The meals have been planned to supply some protein to help switch off hunger, as much slow-releasing carbohydrate as feasible and some fat to provide Essential Fatty Acids. They also contain fruits and vegetables to boost vitamin and mineral intakes and help to keep you physically fit.

While the choice of Love Bites you add to bring the total calories up to your daily requirement is up to you, try to go for fruits and slow-release carbohydrates as often as possible to help keep hunger under control. The slow-release Love Bites are marked with an asterisk (*). It is best to use your Love Bites at the times of day when you particularly feel the need to nibble, although they can also be used to bulk out meals.

The good thing about this diet plan is its flexibility. You can have any breakfast you fancy and can dig into any lunch or dinner that suits you on any of the days. If you want to have exactly the same breakfast, lunch and dinner every day for the 15 days, then it would not matter from a calorie point of view – although it would not supply a good variety of nutrients and could get a tad tedious for your tastebuds!

While Peter Vaughan's lunch and dinner recipes taste sensational and are very simple to throw together, for people who live their lives on the run I've also included some fast options using ready-made sandwiches and evening meals.

The only thing left to say is good luck and enjoy the grub. I can't think of a more lip-smacking and indulgent way to be able to shape up for the beach or bedroom.

quick weekday **breakfasts**

bran and fruit quick start

300 calories

2 g fat

50 g All Bran

30 g chopped dates

1 apple, chopped

200 ml skimmed milk

Tablespoon low-fat yoghurt

Mix together the All Bran, dates and apple. Pour over the milk and top with the yoghurt.

hot croissants

300 calories

10 g fat

25% reduced-fat croissant

200 ml orange juice

100-g pot very low-fat fruit fromage frais

Heat up the croissant, and eat. Follow with the fromage frais and OJ.

fit fix

300 calories
4 g fat

40 g porridge oats
140 ml skimmed milk
40 g ready-to-eat apricots or sultanas

Mix together all ingredients. Microwave for $1^1/_2$ minutes on full power. Stir and allow to stand for a minute. Serve with a bit more milk and a tiny sprinkling of brown sugar.

fruit salad

300 calories
2 g fat

Three fruits of your choice
100-g pot of low-fat yoghurt

Pick three fruits such as a banana, apple and pear and chop. Mix together and serve topped with a yoghurt of your choice. Try 100 g of Total 2% fat greek strained yoghurt with peach.

raspberry muffins

300 calories
10 g fat

ASDA (or other brand)
cranberry/raspberry wholemeal muffin
50 g Philadelphia Light cream cheese

Slice the muffin in half and toast. Serve spread with the cream cheese. You can use a plain wholemeal muffin as an alternative.

honey, oat bran and barley bread

300 calories

8 g fat

2 slices of Vogel's honey,
oat bran and barley bread
(other wholemeal or granary
bread can be used as an alternative)
Low-fat spread and Marmite to taste

Toast the bread. Spread very thinly with low-fat spread and Marmite.

fruit compote on rye

300 calories

7 g fat

Four rye crispbreads
40 g Philadelphia Light
cream cheese
100 g St Michael (or other
brand) blackberry and apple compote

Spread the crispbreads with the cream cheese. Top with the fruit compote.

grab and go **breakfasts**

yoghurt and fruit mix

300 calories
4 g fat

Müller Light yoghurt
large banana
large apple
cappuccino

Eat the yoghurt and fruit separately, or chop the fruit up and top with the yoghurt. Have with a take-away skimmed milk cappuccino.

danone actimel drink

300 calories
8 g fat

Danone Actimel live yoghurt
drink
Wholemeal fruit scone

Drink down the Danone accompanied by the scone and, if you wish, a skimmed milk cappuccino.

desk-top cornflakes

300 calories
3 g fat

Rumbler's Cornflakes (see over)

Banana

100-g pot of very low fat

fruit fromage frais

Rumbler's Cornflakes come complete with a bowl and fresh semi-skimmed milk. Serve with the banana and fromage frais.

leisurely breakfast **treats**

french toast

300 calories

8 g fat

1 egg

pinch cinnamon and brown sugar

2 slices wholemeal or rye bread

Low-fat cooking spray

2 tablespoons very low-fat fromage frais

Slices of fresh peach

Whisk the egg; add the cinnamon and brown sugar. Dip the bread into the egg mix to coat both sides. Spray a non-stick pan with a shot of low-fat cooking spray. Cook for 2 to 3 minutes on either side. While still hot top with the fromage frais and peach slices.

bacon sandwich

300 calories

10 g fat

1 tomato, sliced
40 g (2 small rashers) very lean back bacon
Two slices of bread

Grill or microwave the tomato slices. Grill the bacon. Toast the bread. Hey, presto! Bacon and tomato sarnie!

smoked haddock omelette

300 calories

3 g fat

3 egg whites
salt and pepper
low-fat cooking spray
50 g smoked haddock, flaked
2 slices toasted rye bread
1 tomato, grilled

Whisk the egg whites and add seasoning. Heat a non-stick frying pan and spray with low-fat cooking spray. Pour in the egg mix and shake the pan well. Put the flaked smoked haddock on top, then place under the grill for 3 minutes. Turn out onto a plate. Serve with the bread and tomato.

egg and mushrooms

300 calories
8 g fat

sliced mushrooms
oil or low-fat cooking spray
black pepper
1 egg
teaspoon vinegar
1 slice toast

Spray the sliced mushrooms with low-fat cooking spray or brush very lightly with the oil. Grind over some black pepper and grill. Poach the egg by dropping into brisk boiling water with the teaspoon of vinegar. Drain the egg and serve on the slice of toast surrounded by the mushrooms.

beans on toast

300 calories
3 g fat

1 135-g can of baked beans
2 slices wholemeal toast
1 tomato, grilled
Worcestershire sauce or barbecue sauce to taste

Heat the beans and serve spread over the toast. Top with the grilled tomato. If you fancy you can spice up the beans by adding a dash of Worcestershire or barbecue sauce.

quick lunchtime **fixes**

If you have no time to prepare Peter's mouth-watering lunchtime treats, then don't despair and definitely don't give up. Here are umpteen choices that are fast, convenient and designed to keep you on track. Remember to use Love Bites to bring your total lunchtime calories up to 400 a day.

Either make your own sandwiches, rolls and wraps to take with you to work, or make the most of pre-packed High Street offerings. To whip a sarnie up at home, stick to the proportions listed below. This will provide around 300 calories, and although the fat will vary according to the filling you choose, all are relatively low in total.

home-made sandwiches

Use two slices of fresh bread of your choice (preferably rye) and spread with reduced-fat salad cream. Fill with 65 g of lean chicken, 80 g of roast turkey, 50 g of roast pork or 60 g of roast beef. Add plenty of salad to bulk out the sandwich, and lots of black pepper for extra flavour. If you like fish, then use 50 g canned salmon or 80 g canned tuna in brine. For a cheese sandwich, use 30 g of grated reduced-fat cheddar.

Serve with a 100-calorie Love Bite.

home-made rolls

For a cheddar pickle roll, spread both sides of the roll with pickle and fill with 35 g of grated reduced-fat cheddar mixed with finely chopped spring onion. Cover with slices of cucumber.

Serve with a 100-calorie Love Bite.

Alternatively, have a St Michael granary roll spread with pickle or reduced-fat salad cream and use a slice of lean ham (or turkey or chicken) to fill, along with a sliced tomato.

Serve with a 100-calorie Love Bite.

shop sandwiches

Boots Shapers feta cheese flatbread

287 calories

11 g fat

Plus have a 100-calorie Love Bite.

Boots Shapers spicy Mexican flatbread with kidney beans

297 calories

8 g fat

Plus 100-calorie Love Bite.

Boots Shapers roasted vegetable sandwich

280 calories

4 g fat

Plus 100-calorie Love Bite.

Boots Shapers roast chicken with creamy black pepper
and mayonnaise sandwich

282 calories

10 g fat

Plus 100-calorie Love Bite.

St Michael 95% fat-free lean danish ham salad
sandwich

234 calories

5 g fat

Plus piece of fruit and 100-calorie Love Bite.

St Michael prawn and cocktail sauce on Vitbe bread

232 calories

6 g fat

Plus piece of fruit and 100-calorie Love Bite.

St Michael char-grilled chicken-filled pitta

279 calories

7 g fat

Plus 100-calorie Love Bite.

Waitrose reduced-fat prawn and mayonnaise oatmeal
bread sandwich

289 calories

13 g fat

Plus 100-calorie Love Bite.

Sainsbury's Be Good to Yourself tuna and cucumber sandwich

277 calories

6 g fat

Plus 100-calorie Love Bite.

Sainsbury's Be Good to Yourself prawn cocktail sandwich

299 calories

6 g fat

Plus 100-calorie Love Bite.

Sainsbury's Be Good to Yourself salmon and cucumber sandwich

246 calories

5 g fat

Plus piece of fruit and 100-calorie Love Bite.

Safeway's Healthy Choice roast chicken with yoghurt and cream dressing sandwich

253 calories

6 g fat

Plus piece of fruit and 100-calorie Love Bite.

Safeway's Chinese-style chicken sandwich

288 calories

9 g fat

Plus 100-calorie Love Bite.

Tesco's 95% fat-free egg salad sandwich

245 calories

7 g fat

Plus piece of fruit and 100-calorie Love Bite.

Tesco's 95% fat-free char-grilled chicken and caesar sandwich

270 calories

7 g fat

Plus 100-calorie Love Bite.

Tesco's 95% fat-free salmon and cucumber sandwich

247 calories

6 g fat

Plus piece of fruit and 100-calorie Love Bite.

Tesco's 95% fat-free Yorkshire ham salad sandwich

226 calories

5 g fat

Plus two pieces fruit and 100-calorie Love Bite.

more lunchtime choices

St Michael pasta salad with tuna and sweetcorn

220 calories

6 g fat

Plus piece of fruit and 100-calorie Love Bite.

St Michael sushi packs

291 calories

4 g fat

These come with 4 pieces of raw fish topped with rice and 4 rice sushi rolls.

Plus 100-calorie Love Bite.

Kallo rice cakes with cauldron tomato lentil and basil paté

286 calories

10 g fat

Four rice cakes spread with a 113-g pack of paté

Plus 100-calorie Love Bite.

Baxter's healthy chicken and vegetable soup

300 calories

3 g fat

Will make 300 calories/3 g fat served with a whole-meal roll and an apple.

Plus 100-calorie Love Bite.

Boots Shapers tuna pasta and crunchy vegetable salad box

266 calories

6 g fat

Plus 100 g very low-fat fromage frais and 100-calorie Love Bite.

Boots Shapers mediterranean-style chicken pasta

241 calories

9 g fat

Plus piece of fruit and 100-calorie Love Bite.

baked potatoes

Either make these at home in the microwave or buy from sandwich bars or dedicated baked potato cafés.

A 150-g potato filled with any of the following adds up to approximately 300 calories:

Small can (135 g) baked beans

100 g cottage cheese

40 g chopped ham with some low-fat fromage frais and a tomato

60 g prawns mixed with tablespoon low-fat Thousand Island dressing and 2 tablespoons low-fat yoghurt

40 g grated reduced-fat cheddar

All can be served with a green salad.

Plus 100-calorie Love Bite.

Peter's lunchtime **delights**

salmon and fennel crispbreads

250 calories

6 g fat

7 g fibre

113 mg calcium, 3 mg iron,

2 mg zinc, 21 mg vitamin C, 6

mcg vitamin D

This is a tasty way of transforming tinned salmon into a fast lunchtime treat. The fennel and lemon juice help to balance the richness of the salmon and enhance the flavour. Back in ancient Rome, women wafted fennel under their noses when trying to lose weight. They knew that the aroma helped to switch off hunger. Give it a try before preparing these tasty little morsels for lunch.

Half a bulb of fennel

60 g red tinned salmon (drained)

1 teaspoon horseradish relish

1 teaspoon fresh lemon juice

1 tablespoon fromage frais (virtually fat free)

2 teaspoons freshly chopped chives

Pinch of salt and freshly ground black pepper

4 wholemeal crispbreads

Handful prepared mixed salad leaves

Simply grate the fennel on the coarse side of a sharp grater, into a bowl. Then add the (drained) tinned salmon and mix well using a fork.

Add the horseradish relish, lemon juice, fromage frais and half of the chopped chives. Mix all of the ingredients together well and add a pinch of salt and plenty of freshly ground black pepper.

Spread the salmon mix onto the wholemeal crispbreads just before serving. If you intend to take this lunch to work with you, then separate the salmon mix and crispbreads until you are ready to eat them, or the crispbreads will get soggy.

Serve the crispbreads on a plate and sprinkle with the reserved chopped chives. Garnish with the salad leaves mixed with a little fat-free salad dressing.

Follow with a piece of fruit and a 100-calorie Love Bite.

crab-stuffed coriander pittas

250 calories
2 g fat
7 g fibre
188 mg calcium, 1 mg beta carotene, 6 mg zinc, 42 mg vitamin C, 2 mg vitamin E

This is a quick and simple lunchtime meal that you can make before going to work, as the filling keeps well inside the pitta. You can add as much Tabasco sauce as you like to spice things up.

2 ripe tomatoes
100 g cooked crab meat (either fresh or tinned, drained)
1 tablespoon freshly chopped coriander
1 tablespoon finely chopped spring onions
1 wholemeal pitta bread
A few drops Tabasco sauce
2 teaspoons fresh lemon juice
1 tablespoon fat-free Thousand Island dressing
Cayenne pepper
1 small baby gem lettuce (washed)

Pre-heat grill to maximum.

Chop the tomatoes into small pieces and then add to a mixing bowl with the crabmeat, coriander and spring onions. Mix all of the ingredients together well.

Meanwhile, place the wholemeal pitta under the grill for a minute or two either side, to crisp the surface slightly and open up the inside.

Now add to the crabmeat mixture the Tabasco, lemon juice, Thousand Island dressing and a little pinch of cayenne pepper. Mix until all of the ingredients are thoroughly blended together.

Remove the pitta from the grill and, using a sharp knife, slit open one side and open out the inside to form a pocket. Allow the inside to cool slightly before adding the Baby Gem lettuce leaves, then stuff with the crabmeat filling.

Either serve immediately or store in the fridge until ready to eat.

Follow with a piece of fruit and a 100-calorie Love Bite.

houmous 'light' on toasted rye

300 calories
6 g fat
12 g fibre
168 mg calcium, 2 mg zinc, 5 mg beta carotene, 5 mg vitamin E, 442 mg vitamin C

This is a lighter version of the popular, though fat-laden, houmous dip. Dip any vegetable sticks that take your fancy. Be warned, this recipe has got lots of garlic, which is good for your circulation but not so great for your breath. Make sure anyone you are planning to kiss tonight has some too.

45 g cooked chickpeas
Juice of half a fresh lemon
1 teaspoon crunchy peanut butter
1 teaspoon chopped fresh mint
1 teaspoon mild curry paste
2 cloves garlic
3 tablespoons fromage frais (virtually fat free)
2 large slices rye bread (50 g)
1 carrot, 1 stick celery, 1 green pepper
Salt and pepper to taste

Place the cooked chickpeas in a small blender, liquidizer or food processor and add lemon juice, peanut butter, mint and curry paste. Blend until the ingredients start to break down slightly. Now add 1 well-crushed clove of garlic and add, along with the fromage frais. Continue to blend until a smooth paste starts to form.

Meanwhile, place the rye bread slices into a toaster to crisp; cut the vegetables into thick sticks to dip. Once the rye bread is toasted, rub with a cut clove of fresh garlic (this is optional)!

Once the houmous is smooth and ready, season with a little salt and pepper to taste. Serve the dip in a small bowl with the freshly toasted garlic rye and vegetable sticks. This dip will travel very well, though make sure you cover it securely if you're on the move.

Follow with two 50-calorie Love Bites or one 100-calorie Love Bite.

cashew nut rice salad with mango

350 calories

10 g fat

10 g fibre

5 mg iron, 108 mg vitamin C, 2 mg zinc, 5 mcg selenium, 4 mg vitamin E, 8 mcg vitamin D

This salad is made in minutes and is so easy to whip up and take with you to work. You can buy ready-cooked brown rice in tins, or cook a batch yourself at the beginning of the week, as it keeps well in the fridge or freezer. Resist the temptation to nibble on extra cashews.

Half a tablespoon (15 g) salted cashew nuts
Half a fresh mango (peeled)
Half a red pepper
4 heaped tablespoons cooked brown rice
1 tablespoon chopped chives
Small bunch spring onions finely sliced
1 tablespoon chopped parsley
Juice of half a lemon
Salt and pepper
Lettuce leaves

Heat a small frying pan on a moderate heat and roughly chop the cashew nuts. Place the nuts in the heated frying pan. Heat up gently to release flavour from the nuts – this cuts down on the amount you have to use.

Meanwhile cut the mango flesh into small cubes, along with the red pepper. Mix the two ingredients in a bowl with the cooked brown rice. Now add the chopped chives, spring onions, parsley and lemon juice, and continue to mix. Once the cashew nuts have toasted slightly, mix half of them into the salad and reserve the remainder for garnishing the top.

Season to taste and serve in a suitable serving bowl with some lettuce garnish and, finally, sprinkle with the reserved cashew nuts. Alternatively this salad can be thrown in a suitable sandwich box and whisked off to work with you.

Follow with a 50-calorie Love Bite.

salad niçoise with grilled tuna

250 calories

10 g fat

10 g fibre

5 mg iron, 108 mg calcium, 2 mg zinc, 5 mcg selenium, 4 mg vitamin E, 8 mcg vitamin D

This recipe is meant to be simple, so don't worry if you haven't got a trendy char grill. A normal domestic grill will do. If you can't get fresh tuna then use the same weight of tuna canned in brine. It does the trick and is more economical.

We have skipped the anchovies, since those little fishes can bump up the calories.

1 clove garlic

50 g piece fresh tuna

Salt and freshly ground black pepper

Low-fat cooking spray

1 tablespoon fat-free vinaigrette

2 teaspoons fresh lemon juice

A few leaves torn fresh basil leaves

4 boiled new potatoes

50 g French beans (boiled in salted water and cooled)

Quarter head of shredded iceberg lettuce

2 tomatoes

2 black olives

Pre-heat grill to maximum.

Cut a clove of fresh garlic and rub it all over the piece of tuna. Now season generously with salt and pepper and spray with a little low-fat cooking spray.

Place on a suitable baking tray under the preheated grill for 3 minutes either side. This will be enough to cook the tuna pink. If you prefer it rare, then cook it for just 2 minutes either side.

Meanwhile mix together the dressing, lemon juice and torn basil leaves. Add the new potatoes, French beans, lettuce and tomatoes. Add a little salt and plenty of freshly ground black pepper.

Place some of the salad mixture in the middle of a suitable plate and then place the cooked tuna and any juices on top. Garnish with the olives, either finely sliced or chopped.

Follow with a piece of fruit and a 100-calorie Love Bite.

chicken noodle soup

350 calories
5 g fat
1 g fibre
3 mg iron, 5 mcg selenium

Surprisingly, this soup does not take very long to make. Soups often taste better eaten the day after preparation, but this is so delicious it will be a surprise if it lasts that long. You could easily turn this into a prawn and noodle soup simply by replacing the chicken stock for vegetable and the chicken for 100 g of cooked drained prawns instead.

350 ml kettle-hot water
1 chicken stock cube
100 g skinless chicken breast (finely sliced or cubed)
50 g vermicelli
4 button mushrooms
1 tablespoon finely sliced spring onions
1 clove garlic
1 tablespoon light soya sauce
1 tablespoon chopped coriander
1 large slice rye bread

Bring the hot water and stock cube (in a medium-sized saucepan on a moderate heat) to a simmer. Now add the finely sliced chicken breast meat and the vermicelli. Let the soup gently simmer away for 8 minutes.

Meanwhile finely slice the mushrooms and spring onions, crush the garlic and add all three to the soup.

Add the soya sauce and chopped coriander, and allow the soup to continue to simmer for a couple more minutes. Add a little more soya sauce if you desire a little more of a salty taste, but go easy.

Toast 1 large slice of rye bread and, when the soup is ready, serve immediately with the toasted rye bread.

Follow with a 50-calorie Love Bite.

grilled paprika salmon with a potato-and-grain mustard salad

300 calories

9 g fat

8 g fibre

110 mg calcium, 5 mg iron, 1 mg zinc, 2 mcg selenium, 1 mg beta-carotene, 77 mg vitamin C, omega 3 fatty acids

Although this dish could be used as a dinnertime meal by doubling the amount of potatoes you serve, it is probably best as a quick, refreshing lunchtime dish. If you are not a fan of grain mustard, leave it out or replace it with another flavouring, such as a teaspoon of horseradish.

60 g piece salmon fillet

Salt

1 teaspoon paprika

4 new potatoes (pre-boiled and still hot)

1 teaspoon grain mustard

1 tablespoon chopped parsley

Salt and pepper

2 shallots, peeled and finely chopped

1 tablespoon fat-free salad dressing

1 head chicory lettuce

1 ripe pear

1 teaspoon chopped chives

1 ripe tomato

Pre-heat grill to maximum.

Season the salmon fillet all over with a little salt and all of the paprika. Place on a suitable baking tray and then put under the grill on one side for 6 minutes.

Meanwhile, using a fork, simply crush the hot, cooked potatoes and add the grain mustard, parsley, salt, pepper, shallots and salad dressing. Reserve to one side while you prepare the salad.

Slice the chicory and the pear finely and then mix with the chopped chives. Now chop the tomatoes into small pieces and add to the chicory leaves.

Remove the salmon from the grill to rest for a moment before serving. Serve the chicory and pear salad on a suitable plate, along with the crushed mustard potatoes, then place the cooked salmon fillet on top with the cooking juices drizzled around.

Follow with two 50-calorie Love Bites or one 100-calorie Love Bite.

muffin pizzas with quorn and tomato

400 calories

11 g fat

6 g fibre

345 mg vitamin C, 3 mg iron,

2 mg zinc, 25 mcg selenium

Delicious hot or cold, you can whip up pizzas the night before and take them to work the following day. Make the effort to buy wholemeal muffins – they will fill you up and satisfy you more.

1 wholemeal muffin

1 tablespoon tomato purée, 1 tablespoon passata

1 clove crushed garlic

A few leaves freshly torn basil leaves

Salt, sugar and freshly ground black pepper

6 button mushrooms

50 g Quorn (chopped into little pieces)

1 slice wholemeal bread

30 g grated reduced-fat cheddar cheese (grated)

A handful prepared salad leaves

2 teaspoons fat-free dressing

1 slice rye bread

Pre-heat oven to 450°F/230°C/Gas Mark 8.

Slice the muffin horizontally to make two separate halves; place on a baking tray. Mix together the tomato purée with the passata, the crushed garlic clove and the basil leaves. Season with salt, pepper and a pinch of sugar and then spread this mixture on top of each muffin slice.

Slice the mushrooms finely and sprinkle on top of the tomato mix, along with the chopped Quorn.

Chop the slice of wholemeal bread into little pieces and then mix with the grated cheese. This can be placed on top of the muffins ready for baking.

The muffin pizzas will take about 10 minutes to bake in the pre-heated oven. Meanwhile, prepare your salad leaves with a little dressing and toast the slice of rye bread. This can then be cut into little croutons to give your salad an interesting texture.

Serve the muffin pizzas when ready with salad and rye bread croutons.

penne pasta salad with prawns and lemon dressing

250 calories

3 g fat

3 g fibre

187 mg calcium, 3 mg zinc, 1 mg beta carotene, 2 mg vitamin E, 31 mg vitamin C

This is a brilliant lunch box salad, so there's no excuses for straying off the diet plan just because you're always on the go at work. It's a light yet satisfying salad and will help keep you going until dinnertime. Swap the prawns and substitute the same weight in cooked (skinless) chicken or turkey, if you prefer.

1 teaspoon Dijon mustard

2 teaspoons lemon juice

1 teaspoon tomato purée

1 tablespoon fat-free Thousand Island dressing

A few drops Tabasco sauce

Salt, sugar and freshly ground black pepper

Quarter of a cucumber

2 ripe plum tomatoes

115 g cooked penne pasta

100 g cooked drained prawns

1 tablespoon chopped chives

In a large bowl mix the mustard, lemon juice, tomato purée, Thousand Island dressing, Tabasco, a pinch of sugar and a little salt and freshly ground black pepper.

Cut the cucumber and tomatoes into small dice and add them to the mustard/tomato purée mixture. Then add the penne pasta and the cooked prawns and mix well with half of the chopped chives.

Season the salad with plenty of freshly ground black pepper and a little more salt if necessary. Serve in a suitable serving bowl or a portable sandwich tub. Sprinkle with the remaining chopped chives for garnish.

Follow with a piece of fruit and a 100-calorie Love Bite.

curried chickpea soup with mint

300 calories

5 g fat

8 g fibre

166 mg calcium, 7 mg iron,

4 mg vitamin E

Soups are great fillers for lunchtime and this one is no exception. It can be prepared on the day, the night before or well ahead and frozen at the start of your 15-day plan. You can change the spices in this recipe to suit your palate! Buy a small thermos flask and take hot soup and rye bread with you to work for lunch.

Half a medium onion (peeled)
Low-fat cooking spray
120 g tinned chickpeas (drained)
Half a ground cumin
Half teaspoon turmeric
2 teaspoons mild curry paste
2 cloves garlic (crushed)
100 g tinned chopped tomatoes
600 ml vegetable stock (use a stock cube)
2 large slices rye bread
Salt and pepper
1 teaspoon fromage frais (virtually fat free)
A small bunch fresh mint leaves

Place a moderate/large saucepan on to heat and, whilst it is heating, chop the onion finely.

When the pan is hot, spray in a few shots of low fat cooking spray, add the onions and sauté gently. Once the onions have softened slightly, add the chickpeas, cumin, turmeric, curry paste and crushed garlic.

Now add the tinned tomatoes and vegetable stock, and

bring to a gentle boil. Allow the soup to simmer for 10–12 minutes and then place it in a food processor or liquidizer and blend until smooth.

Toast the slices of rye bread ready to serve with the chickpea soup. Once the soup is well blended, season to taste and serve hot in a suitable bowl.

Garnish the soup with a small spoonful of fromage frais and a sprinkle of freshly chopped mint.

Follow with two 50-calorie Love Bites or one 100-calorie Love Bite.

chicken caesar salad

350 calories
14 g fat
3 g fibre
3 mg iron, 3 mg zinc, 9 mcg selenium, 1 mcg vitamin D, 2 mg vitamin E

Would you believe that, even though you are currently on the *Sexy Thing* diet, you can still enjoy the pleasures of a good Caesar salad? The secret of a great Caesar salad is to make it just before you want to eat it – this way the lettuce keeps crisp and the croutons stay crunchy. There is little worse than limp lettuce.

2 large slices rye bread

Low-fat cooking spray

1 small free-range egg, hard boiled

Half a clove crushed garlic

1 tablespoon 'Weight Watchers Caesar style' dressing

2 teaspoons lemon juice

Salt and pepper

65 g cooked skinless chicken breast (sliced finely)

1 whole clove garlic

1 head Cos lettuce (washed and cut into chunks)

10 g grated fresh Parmesan cheese

Freshly ground black pepper

Pre-heat grill to maximum.

Spray the slices of rye bread with a little of the low-fat cooking spray and place under the grill to toast thoroughly on both sides.

Take the shell off the hard-boiled egg and spoon the contents into a mixing bowl. Add the crushed garlic, Caesar-style dressing, lemon juice and salt and pepper.

Whisk the dressing well and add the finely sliced cooked chicken. Leave to marinade slightly. Remove the rye bread from the grill and rub with a freshly-cut clove of garlic.

The rye toast can now be cut into dice-size pieces, add half to the chicken and reserve the rest for garnish. Add the Cos lettuce to the chicken and dressing and mix lightly.

Serve in a suitable bowl with the reserved croutons on top. Sprinkle with Parmesan and freshly ground black pepper.

Follow with a 50-calorie Love Bite.

bacon and egg crumpets

> 400 calories
> 13 g fat
> 6 g fibre
> 4 mg iron, 3 mg zinc, 2 mg
> vitamin E, 1 mcg vitamin D,
> 19 mg vitamin C

There's nothing like a bit of crumpet, and if you've never tried them dipped in egg and mustard then you've missed a delight. Make them when your intended pops round and they will find the beautiful aromas from your kitchen simply too much to resist.

2 (56 g) rashers lean back bacon (all rind removed)
2 large flat mushrooms
Salt and black pepper
Low-fat cooking spray
1 egg (well beaten)
100 ml skimmed milk
2 teaspoons Dijon mustard
2 crumpets
1 large beef tomato (sliced)

Pre-heat the grill to maximum.

Place the trimmed bacon on a wire grill tray, along with the flat mushrooms. Season the mushrooms with salt and pepper and spray on a little low-fat cooking spray.

Meanwhile beat the egg with the milk, mustard and a little salt and pepper in a large mixing bowl. Place the two crumpets in the bowl and leave them to soak the mixture up for a few minutes.

Place a non-stick frying pan on a moderate heat and spray in a couple of shots of low-fat cooking spray. Place the egg-soaked crumpets in and leave to cook very gently for 2 minutes either side.

Remove the bacon and mushrooms from the grill. When the crumpets are ready, simply serve on a suitable plate with the bacon on top. Garnish with the sliced tomato and grilled mushrooms. Ketchup is also allowed for the real addicts!

broccoli and almond soup

> 300 calories
> 13 g fat
> 8 g fibre
> 192 mg calcium, 8 mg iron,
> 3 mg zinc, 15 mcg selenium,
> 1 mg beta-carotene, 8 mg vit-
> amin E, 103 mg vitamin C

Here's an easy-to-make soup that also freezes well. With a little forward planning you can take it to work or have it at home, hot or cold. Whichever way you fancy. Don't get carried away with the almonds – you don't need many for this recipe and when blended into the soup a little goes a long way.

Low-fat cooking spray

Half a head broccoli

Half a small potato (peeled)

Half an onion

20 g flaked almonds

1 clove garlic

A small bunch fresh chives

A few sprigs fresh thyme

600 ml vegetables stock (use a stock cube)

Salt and pepper

A slice fresh wholemeal bread

Place a saucepan on a moderate heat and then spray a little low-fat cooking spray into the pan. Break the broccoli up into very small pieces and chop the potato up into a small dice.

Finely slice the onion and sauté in the hot pan, adding the broccoli and potatoes. Continue to cook for a couple of minutes. Add the flaked almonds, garlic and chives.

Continue to cook on a moderate heat for a minute or so, add the thyme and stock and bring to the boil. Reduce the heat and cook on a gentle simmer for 12–14 minutes.

Once the soup has simmered, carefully pour the contents into a food processor or liquidizer and blend until smooth. Season to taste and then pour into a suitable serving bowl or thermos flask and serve with a slice of wholemeal bread.

Follow with two 50-calorie Love Bites or one 100-calorie Love Bite.

sardines on toast with a twist

300 calories

8 g fat

7 g fibre

334 mg calcium, 6 mg iron, 3 mg zinc, 14 mcg selenium, 1 mg beta-carotene, 3 mg vitamin E, 48 mg vitamin C

OK, I know, this dish doesn't sound very sexy – but don't be fooled. Tasty packages can be well disguised, and here's a good example. A rapid and easy meal, it knocks spots off your average sardines on toast and is bulging with that all-important male mineral zinc. Inject some heat into those sardines and enjoy!

1 large slice rye bread

50 g tinned sardines (drained)

1 teaspoon Dijon mustard

2 teaspoon chopped chives

1 teaspoon lemon juice

Freshly ground black pepper

2 ripe tomatoes

1 slice wholemeal bread

2 teaspoons chopped parsley

1 teaspoon grain mustard

Low-fat cooking spray

Salad leaves to serve

Pre-heat the grill to maximum.

Place the slice of rye bread under the grill and toast either side. Meanwhile mix the drained sardines with the Dijon mustard, chopped chives, lemon juice and plenty of freshly ground black pepper using a fork.

Once the rye bread is well toasted, cut the tomatoes into thin slices and arrange on top of the toast. Evenly spread the sardine mixture on top of the tomatoes.

In a food processor or liquidizer break the wholemeal bread into small pieces and pulse until rough breadcrumbs form. Put the crumbs into a bowl and mix with the chopped parsley and grain mustard. Once the breadcrumb mixture is thoroughly combined, spread on top of the sardines, spray with low-fat cooking spray and place under the grill for 3–4 minutes.

The sardines on toast are ready once the breadcrumb mixture has turned golden brown and crunchy in texture. Serve immediately on a suitable serving plate with a mixture of washed salad leaves.

Follow with two 50-calorie Love Bites or one 100-calorie Love Bite.

'You Sexy Thing' BLT

300 calories
10 g fat
6 g fibre
4 mg iron, 3 mg zinc, 27 mcg
selenium, 1 mg beta carotene,
23 mg vitamin C

The one overwhelming point about the *You Sexy Thing!* diet is that you don't have to miss out on all of life's goodies. And that includes the famous BLT sandwich. With just a little thought you can turn this traditionally fat-laden sandwich oozing with mayo and streaky fatty bacon into a piece of real lean cuisine. Lighten up with the fat and dig into this deliciously tasty toasted BLT.

70 g back bacon (all rind removed) approximately 3 large rashers
2 slices wholemeal bread
1 teaspoon Dijon mustard
1 dessertspoon reduced-fat salad cream
A handful shredded iceberg lettuce
Salt and black pepper
2 ripe tomatoes

Pre-heat grill to maximum.

Place the bacon under the grill to cook thoroughly for approximately 3 minutes either side.

Meanwhile place the wholemeal bread under the grill as well, to toast either side. This is optional. Omit it if you don't want your sandwich toasted.

Add the Dijon mustard to the reduced-fat salad cream and mix well. Add the shredded iceberg to this mixture and season to taste with salt and black pepper.

Remove the toasted bread and place the shredded iceberg on both sides, then cut the tomatoes into thin slices and place them on as well. Remove the grilled bacon and place on one side of the bread. Press both slices of bread together and apply a slight weight to force both sides to stick before slicing.

Slice the sandwich either in halves or into quarters. Serve immediately while the toast and bacon are both still warm.

dinners in a **dash**

Look for the reduced-fat ready meals available from supermarkets. For example, check out some of the following – and serve with suggestions to bring the meal's total calories up to 400.

St Michael 95% fat-free prawn rogan josh

165 calories

7 g fat

Serve with a Sharwood's mini naan bread or 50 g quick-cook rice.

Plus 50-calorie Love Bite for pudding.

Tesco's 97% fat-free steak chasseur

194 calories

6 g fat per serving

Serve with large baked potato and peas.

Plus 100-calorie Love Bite for pudding.

ASDA sliced beef and vegetable fillers

165 calories

5 g fat

Serve with two ASDA ready-to-bake Yorkshire puddings and a large baked potato.

Plus 50-calorie Love Bite for pudding.

Waitrose cottage pie

318 calories

12 g fat

Serve with green beans.

Plus 50-calorie Love Bite for pudding.

Respect's organic vegetable lasagne

291 calories

11 g fat

Serve with a green salad.

Plus 100-calorie Love Bite for pudding.

Tesco's sweet and sour chicken

287 calories

4 g fat per pack

Serve with 150 g cooked rice.

Plus 100-calorie Love Bite for pudding.

Hard Rock Café veggie burgers by Morningstar Farms

167 calories

8 g fat

Serve with a hamburger bun, some sliced tomato, gherkin and reduced-fat salad cream.

Plus 50-calorie Love Bite for pudding.

Quorn sausages

116 calories

4 g fat

Serve two grilled Quorn sausages with half a pack of St Michael 95% Fat-free Mashed Potato, with Carrot, Swede and Butter and a grilled tomato.

Plus 100-calorie Love Bite for pudding.

Weight Watchers chicken tikka balti

234 calories

5 g fat

Serve with two microwaved Sharwood's pappadoms.

Plus 100-calorie Love Bite for pudding.

St Michael tuna and sweetcorn pie

240 calories

7 g fat

Serve with peas and carrots.

Plus 100-calorie Love Bite for pudding.

ASDA chilli con carne fillers

209 calories

3 g fat

Serve with a warm flour tortilla flatbread and salad.

Plus 50-calorie Love Bite for pudding.

Risso gallo quattro formaggi risotto

300 calories

5 g fat

Make a serving using ¹/₃ of the pack.

Serve with a large basil and tomato salad.

Plus 50-calorie Love Bite for pudding.

Tesco's 98% fat-free tuna and pasta bake

281 calories

5 g fat

Serve with a green salad.

Plus 100-calorie Love Bite for pudding.

St Michael haddock and cauliflower cheese

195 calories

6 g fat

Serve with broccoli and a hot roll.

Plus 100-calorie Love Bite for pudding.

Weight Watchers shepherd's pie

241 calories

7 g fat

Serve with a large helping of green beans and two tablespoons of sweetcorn.

Plus 100-calorie Love Bite for pudding.

St Michael ricotta and spinach cannelloni

> 270 calories
>
> 5 g fat

Serve with a green salad.

Plus 100-calorie Love Bite for pudding.

Weight Watchers ocean pie with cod

> 254 calories
>
> 8 g fat

Serve with canned (40 g) sweetcorn.

Plus 100-calorie Love Bite for pudding.

St Michael sundried tomato and basil chicken escalopes

> 135 calories
>
> 3 g fat

Serve one escalope with 200 g of cooked tagliatelle and a mixed salad.

Plus 50-calorie Love Bite for pudding.

Safeway's spaghetti bolognese

> Per pack:
>
> 284 calories
>
> 9 g fat

Serve with a salad and 100-calorie Love Bite.

Safeway's beef and ale cobbler

> Per half-pack serving:
>
> 377 calories
>
> 14 g fat

Serve with some green beans.

Safeway's macaroni cheese

> Per 300-g pack:
>
> 320 calories
>
> 11 g fat

Serve with a large mixed salad and 50-calorie Love Bite.

Peter's delectable **dinners**

Moroccan chickpea casserole with couscous

> 350 calories
>
> 5 g fat
>
> 7 g fibre
>
> 139 mg calcium, 8 mg iron, 1 mg zinc, 6 mcg selenium, 72 mcg folate, 36 mg vitamin C, 3 mg vitamin E

A light and spicy taste of the exotic, this North African dish will satiate even the largest appetite. Easy to prepare in advance, if you fancy it – whip some up before starting the 15-day plan and freeze a batch for later.

Half a medium onion

50 g button mushrooms

Low-fat cooking spray

1 clove garlic (crushed)

90 g cooked chickpeas (drained)

Half teaspoon ground cumin and coriander

2 teaspoons tomato purée

100 g chopped cooked tinned tomatoes

50 g sultanas (soaked in 100 ml kettle-hot water)

550 ml hot vegetable stock (use a stock cube)

6 level tablespoons couscous

Salt and cayenne pepper

1 tablespoon chopped parsley

Heat a suitably sized saucepan on the stove. Finely chop the onion and finely slice the mushrooms. When the saucepan is moderately hot, add a little of the low-fat cooking spray and then the onions and sliced mushrooms. Continue to cook until the vegetables soften slightly.

After a minute or so add the garlic, chickpeas, cumin and coriander. Continue to sauté until the flavours of the spices really start to release themselves. Now add the tomato purée, cooked tinned tomatoes, sultanas (with their water) and 250 ml of the vegetable stock. Bring the casserole to the boil and turn down the heat to simmer gently for 10 minutes.

Meanwhile put the couscous in a saucepan over a high heat and cook dry for 2–4 minutes. Pour on the remaining 300 ml of the vegetable stock, turn off the heat and cover with a tight-fitting lid or clingfilm. Leave the couscous to absorb all of the stock for 5—6 minutes before serving.

Once the chickpea casserole has simmered for 10 minutes, remove from the heat, season to taste and add the chopped parsley. Serve the cooked couscous on a suitably sized plate and then spoon the chickpea casserole on top.

Follow with a 50-calorie Love Bite.

chicken teriyaki

400 calories

7 g fat

4 g fibre

2 mg zinc, 6 mg beta-carotene,

27 mg vitamin C

Here is an easy-to-make, no fuss, tasty teriyaki sauce to smother a lean chicken breast. You could try making extra sauce to use for other dishes. Whip up the teriyaki sauce in advance; you'll find that it keeps well.

Pan of salted water

1 100-g breast skinless chicken

Salt and pepper

Low-fat cooking spray

1 tablespoon muscavado sugar

1 tablespoon soya sauce

1 tablespoon dry sherry

50 g egg noodles (uncooked weight)

4 spring onions

2 grated carrots

Pre-heat grill to maximum.

Bring a pan of salted water to the boil; leave to simmer.

Meanwhile season the chicken lightly with salt and pepper and place onto a baking tray. Spray with low-fat cooking spray and then place under the grill to cook for 5 minutes either side.

Place the sugar, soya sauce and sherry into a medium pan and slowly bring to the boil. Be careful not to over-boil this mixture. Once the sauce has come to the boil, turn off the heat.

Simply brush or spoon a little of the teriyaki sauce onto the chicken as it cooks under the grill.

Plunge the egg noodles into the boiling water and cook as per the instructions on the packet. Finely slice or chop the spring onions and mix with the grated carrots.

Once the noodles are cooked, drain and mix with the grated vegetables and a little more of the teriyaki sauce. Serve immediately and slice the cooked chicken on top. Drizzle any remaining cooking juices and extra sauce over the chicken.

baked sweet potato with crunchy bacon topping

350 calories

7 g fat

8 g fibre

100 mg calcium, 4 mg iron, 3 mg zinc, 15 mcg selenium, 8 mg beta-carotene, 10 mg vitamin E, 46 mg vitamin C

If you've not tried sweet potato before then you must give it a go. This recipe is a nice way of trying it for first-time tasters. The crunchy texture of the bacon topping marries well with the smooth texture of the potato flesh. If it's easier, use a normal baking potato for this recipe, following the method outlined below.

60 g lean back bacon (all rind removed)
150 g yellow sweet potato (washed)
1 slice wholemeal bread
1 tablespoon chopped chives
1 teaspoon grain mustard
1 teaspoon Dijon mustard
1 shallot (finely chopped)
Salt and pepper
1 bowl prepared mixed salad leaves
A little fat-free salad dressing

Pre-heat grill to maximum.

Place the lean back bacon under the grill to cook for 4–5 minutes. Meanwhile wrap the sweet potato in absorbent paper and then place in the microwave on high for 8 minutes. (If you've not got a microwave, then really you need to bake the potato in advance for about 2 hours.)

While the bacon and potato are cooking, prepare the crunchy topping. Simply chop the wholemeal bread into tiny pieces and mix with the chopped chives, mustards and finely chopped shallot.

Once the bacon is cooked, chop into small pieces. Mix the bacon with the chopped bread mixture. When the sweet potato is cooked, remove and slice in half horizontally. Season with salt and pepper and then spoon on the breadcrumb topping.

Place the sweet potato under the grill and cook until the bacon topping turns a crunchy brown texture. Serve immediately with a pile of mixed salad leaves and a little fat-free salad dressing.

Follow with a 50-calorie Love Bite.

steamed salmon with sautéed sprouting beans

300 calories

13 g fat

9 g fibre

146 mg calcium, 6 mg iron, 2 mg zinc, 38 mg vitamin C, omega 3 fatty acids

Sprouted beans are delicious and nutritious. Sprout your own or look for them in supermarkets. They are becoming increasingly available in larger stores. Served with salmon that has been steamed to retain its delicate flavour, there are few tastier partners for your evening meal.

Pan of water
90 g skinless salmon fillet

Salt and freshly ground black pepper

2 slices lemon

Low-fat cooking spray

90 g sprouting beans

2 cloves crushed garlic

1 tablespoon balsamic vinegar

100 g beansprouts

1 tablespoon chopped parsley

Bring a pan of water to the boil and either place a colander or sieve on top, or a proper steamer attachment.

Season the salmon with salt and plenty of freshly ground black pepper. Top with lemon slices, wrap the salmon in tin foil and then place the parcel into the steamer or colander. Cover with a lid to help keep the heat in and steam for 5 minutes.

Meanwhile place a large frying pan on a high heat. As soon as the pan is hot, spray in a little low-fat cooking spray and then add the sprouting beans. Sauté quickly and add the crushed garlic and balsamic vinegar.

Allow the vinegar to reduce until it reaches a sticky consistency, then add the beansprouts. Continue to cook for a minute, then add the chopped parsley. Serve onto a suitably sized serving plate.

Remove the salmon from the tin foil. Remove any lemon slices stuck to it. Place the salmon on top of the sprouting beans-and-vinegar mixture and serve.

Follow with a 100-calorie Love Bite.

chicken salad with horseradish dressing

300 calories

5 g fat

4 g fibre

83 mg calcium, 2 mg iron, 1 mg beta-carotene, 2 mg vita-min E, 55 mg vitamin C

If you're in a hurry and fancy a salad, this is the one for you. You will be amazed how horseradish dressing enhances the taste of cold chicken. When working late, take this dish with you to head off the vending machine munchies. Planning ahead means there is no room for excuses.

800 g cooked skinless chicken breast meat

Salt, paprika and freshly ground black pepper

1 tablespoon fat-free salad dressing

10 cherry tomatoes

5-cm length cucumber diced

200 g medium potatoes (boiled or steamed in their skins)

1 eating apple (peeled and cubed)

1 little Gem lettuce

2 teaspoons horseradish relish

2 teaspoons lemon juice

2 tablespoons fromage frais (virtually fat-free)

Cut the cooked chicken meat into dice-sized pieces and then place in a bowl with a little salt, pepper and pinch of paprika.

Add the salad dressing and mix well.

Slice the cherry tomatoes in half and add them and the diced cucumber to the chicken. Slice the potatoes and add to the mixture along with the cubed apple and shredded Baby Gem lettuce.

Serve on some whole leaves of prepared Baby Gem.

For the sauce, mix the horseradish relish with the lemon juice and fromage frais. Add a little salt and pepper and mix well. Drizzle the dressing over the chicken salad and serve.

Follow with a 100-calorie Love Bite.

tofu and noodle soup

350 calories
9 g fat
9 g fibre
549 mg calcium, 6 mg iron, 3 mg zinc, 12 mcg selenium, 8 mg beta-carotene, 3 mg vitamin E, 129 mg vitamin C

This 'one-pot wonder' makes a great light supper dish. Use any type of noodle for the broth, but try if you can to find some buckwheat or 'Soba' noodles, as it will be worth the extra flavour. Don't be put off by tofu. If you've never had it, now's the time to give it a whirl. If you've had it before and found it bland, then give it one last try. In this recipe the tofu absorbs the flavours of the aromatic broth, turning it into a tasty treat.

Pan of salted water

50 g noodles (uncooked weight)

600 ml vegetable stock (use two stock cubes)

1 slice ginger

120 g button mushrooms, wiped

120 g carrots (peeled and cut into fine sticks)

120 g broccoli florets

80 g pressed tofu cut into approximately 5-mm slices

1 tablespoon freshly chopped coriander

3 spring onions (finely sliced)

A little soya sauce

Bring a pan of salted water to the boil and cook the noodles as instructed on the packet. Meanwhile, place another pan on the stove with the vegetable stock and slice of ginger.

Bring the vegetable stock to a gentle simmer and add the mushrooms, carrots and broccoli. Once the vegetables are about 80% cooked, add the slices of tofu.

Once the noodles are cooked, drain them and pour into a suitable serving bowl. Add the coriander and spring onions to the vegetable stock and tofu broth, then ladle this soup onto the hot noodles in the bowl.

Drizzle a few drops of soya sauce on top for seasoning and garnish.

Follow with a 50-calorie Love Bite.

mackerel and mango salad

350 calories

11 g fat

9 g fibre

129 mg calcium, 5 mg iron, 2 mg zinc, 15 mcg selenium, 3 mg beta-carotene, 4 mg vitamin E, 115 mg vitamin C, 9 mcg vitamin D, omega 3 fatty acids

This salad might sound weird, but in fact it is delicious. The mackerel is best served warm, as more flavour is released. Rich in essential fatty acids, this oily fish enhances circulation and helps the body cope with a racing pulse.

50 g smoked peppered mackerel

Half a ripe mango

Half a fresh lime

Half a teaspoon mild horseradish relish

Half a teaspoon Dijon mustard

8 cherry tomatoes, cut in half

2-inch length cucumber

A small bunch chopped chives

Small bowl assorted salad leaves

Wholemeal pitta bread

Pre-heat the grill to maximum.

Using a sharp knife, remove the skin and any loose bones from the cooked mackerel fillet. Place the fish on a suitable tray under the grill for 4 minutes to warm up.

Meanwhile, peel and slice the mango thinly and squeeze over the lime juice. This will help keep the colour and improve the flavour.

In a mixing bowl, add the horseradish, mustard and mango with any excess lime juice. Cut the cherry tomatoes in half and cube the cucumber into dice-sized pieces.

Mix the cucumber and cherry tomatoes with the mango and dressing. Add in the salad leaves. Sprinkle with a few chopped chives, reserving a few for garnish.

Toast the pitta bread under the grill on both sides. Cut into 'soldiers'.

Serve the salad on a suitable plate and then gently break the mackerel fillet up using a fork. Sprinkle this over the top of the salad and then, finally, sprinkle with the remaining chives.

Follow with a 50-calorie Love Bite.

grilled pork escalopes with parsley and mustard mash

300 calories
4 g fat
5 g fibre
387 mg calcium, 3 mg iron, 3 mg zinc, 102 mg vitamin C, 1 mg vitamin E

Pork chops and mash are the perfect dining partners, so dig in. We have swapped fatty chops for lean pork escalopes, and replaced butter in the mash with grain mustard to give it a kick and set the taste buds tingling.

150 g peeled red skinned potatoes

70 g lean pork escalopes

Salt and freshly ground black pepper

1 teaspoon runny honey

1 teaspoon Dijon mustard

200 ml skimmed milk

Salt and cayenne pepper

2 teaspoons grain mustard

1 teaspoon Dijon mustard

Selection of steamed vegetables to serve

1 tablespoon chopped fresh parsley

Pre-heat the grill to maximum.

Place the potatoes in a pan of salted water. Bring the pan to the boil and cook for 20 minutes until soft.

Meanwhile, generously season the pork with salt and pepper and then place on a suitable grill tray. Mix the honey with the Dijon mustard and spread on top of the pork. Place the tray under the grill and cook for 10 minutes without turning the pork over.

Drain and return the potatoes to the saucepan and start to mash whilst adding the milk. Season the potatoes with salt and a pinch of cayenne pepper and then add the grain and

Dijon mustard to the mash. If you would like the mash a little smoother, then add more milk, but don't allow it to become too runny.

Steam the vegetables you would like to serve with the pork, such as carrots, green beans, etc.

Remove the pork from the grill and reserve any cooking juices to serve with the meat. At the last moment add a little chopped parsley to the mash and serve on a suitably warm plate. Place the meat on top of the mash and serve with any steamed vegetables you desire.

Follow with a 100-calorie Love Bite.

red kidney bean pulao

400 calories

3 g fat

12 g fibre

6 mg iron, 2 mg zinc, 1 mg vitamin E

Pulao is the South American word for stew, and this version is intended for the seriously spicy among you. Stick with basmati rice for the best taste and texture, and remember it releases energy slowly for the night ahead.

5 level tablespoons Basmati rice
Low-fat cooking spray
Half a cinnamon stick, 1 clove, 2 green cardamom pods

Half an onion sliced

Half a teaspoon freshly grated ginger

Pinch chilli powder

Pinch turmeric

1 clove garlic, crushed

Half teaspoon garam masala

60 g frozen peas

60 g cauliflower florets

1 carrot, sliced

1 courgette, sliced

80 g cooked red kidney beans

Half a tablespoon lemon juice

1 tablespoon fresh chopped coriander leaves

salt

300 ml water

Wash the rice in a large bowl of cold water and leave to soak while you prepare the other ingredients. Heat a suitable saucepan on a moderate heat and add some low-fat cooking spray. Add the cinnamon, cloves and cardamom and cook for about 1 minute.

Add the chopped onion and fry gently for a further 2 minutes. Add the ginger, chilli powder, turmeric, garlic and garam masala, followed by the peas and cauliflower. Continue to cook gently and then add the carrot and courgette slices.

Drain the rice and put it, along with the kidney beans, into the pan with the vegetables. Stir gently and then add the lemon juice, fresh coriander, a little salt and 300 ml of water.

Turn down the heat and cover with a lid.

Leave until all the water has been absorbed and the rice is cooked, about 12–15 minutes. Let the Pulao settle for 5 minutes before serving a generous helping for dinner.

spicy bulgur wheat pilaff with apricots

400 calories
3 g fat
7 g fibre
7 mg iron, 2 mg zinc, 6 mcg selenium, 243 mg calcium

This is a quick dinner dish that takes only minutes but tastes as though you've spent hours slaving over a hot stove. The combination of cereal and pulses makes an excellent source of protein if you are cutting down on the meat, and combined with the apricots and spinach supplies plenty of mighty minerals to keep up your strength.

Low-fat cooking spray
50 g bulgur wheat
Half a finely chopped onion
Pinch ground cinnamon
25 g raisins
50 g dried apricots
300 ml vegetable stock
A large packet fresh baby spinach leaves
A bunch fresh basil leaves

50 g cooked chickpeas

Half a teaspoon chilli sauce or Tabasco sauce

Juice of half a lemon

Zest of half a lemon

Whole nutmeg

In a saucepan add a little low-fat cooking spray and then the bulgur wheat and chopped onion. Cook gently and add the cinnamon, raisins and apricots.

Once the ingredients are well mixed in with the bulgur wheat, add the vegetable stock and turn down the heat to low. Cover with a lid and allow the bulgur wheat to absorb all of the liquid. This will take about 6 minutes.

Shred a little of the spinach and all of the basil leaves and add them, along with the chickpeas, to the cooked bulgur wheat. Mix in thoroughly along with the hot chilli/Tabasco sauce, lemon juice and zest.

Bring a pan of water to the boil and place the rest of the spinach in a steamer to cook.

Once the mixture is well-combined and warm, serve immediately on a suitable plate with some steamed spinach. To add a little extra taste, simply grate over a little fresh nutmeg.

spicy rice 'n' fish cakes

300 calories

8 g fat

4 g fibre

169 mg calcium, 3 mg iron,
2 mg zinc, 10 mcg vitamin D,
51 mg vitamin C, omega 3
fatty acids

Fish cakes are always popular, and you can add virtually any spices you like to them. It's really important to use dry spices, so that as you cook them they release their flavours. Tinned salmon is the fish in these fish cakes, but you can use any other, such as sardines or tuna.

150 g potatoes

Pan of salted water

Low-fat cooking spray

Half a medium onion, peeled and chopped

Half teaspoon ground cumin and coriander

Pinch ground mace

80 g tinned pink salmon

Few leaves fresh coriander

Small bunch chopped chives

Few drops Tabasco

2 tablespoons cooked basmati rice

Salt and pepper

Bag assorted salad leaves
Fat-free dressing

Peel and chop the potatoes into a pan of salted water. Bring to the boil and cook until soft. Meanwhile, heat a non-stick frying pan and add a little low-fat cooking spray.

Cook the chopped onion in the pan with the ground cumin, coriander and mace. Once the onion is soft, add the drained tinned salmon and remove from the heat.

Drain the potatoes when cooked and then, using a fork, crush the potatoes and combine them with the salmon mixture. Chop the fresh coriander and chives and combine these with the Tabasco and basmati rice; add everything into the potato mixture. Season it generously with salt and freshly ground black pepper. The mixture should be firm enough to mould into little cake shapes, or you can make one large one.

Clean the non-stick pan and replace on the heat with a little more low-fat cooking spray. Place the fish/potato cakes in to cook on a moderate heat for 2–3 minutes either side.

Mix the salad leaves with dressing and serve them on a suitable plate. Once the potato cakes are lightly coloured, serve them straight away alongside the salad.

Follow with a 100-calorie Love Bite.

rice noodle stir-fry with shitake mushrooms

400 calories

4 g fat

7 g fibre

135 mg calcium, 7 mg iron, 3 mg zinc, 14 mcg selenium, 5 mg carotene, 199 mcg folate, 79 mg vitamin C

Rice noodles are a great idea if you fancy a change from the usual varieties. There may seem like a lot of chilli in this dish, but it tastes great – and they say chillies help to raise your body metabolic rate and the rate at which you burn up calories. Search out some shitake mushrooms if you can, they have a lovely deep flavour, although standard ones will also be fine.

Pan of salted water
Low-fat cooking spray
55 g lean pork escalope
Salt and pepper
2 tablespoons white wine vinegar
1 tablespoon castor sugar
1 red chilli
50 g rice noodles (dry weight)
150 g shitake mushrooms
2 sliced spring onions
60 g mangetout

1 carrot, peeled and grated
1 tablespoon soya sauce
150 g beansprouts
1 tablespoon chopped coriander

Bring a pan of salted water to the boil, then leave to simmer. Meanwhile, heat a non-stick frying pan on the stove and add a little low-fat cooking spray. Cut the pork escalope into thin strips and season lightly with salt and pepper.

Once the pan is hot, add the pork and cook until the strips of meat are thoroughly cooked. Place the cooked pork on some absorbent paper, then clean the pan and return to the stove.

Mix the white wine vinegar, sugar and chopped chilli together in a small pan and bring to the boil. Now bring the pan of water back to the boil, plunge the noodles in, cook according to the directions on the packet, then drain. Leave the noodles to one side ready to add to the stir-fry.

Add a little more low-fat cooking spray to the pan and then throw in the shitake mushrooms, sliced onions, mangetout and grated carrot. Let the vegetables cook for a couple of minutes and then add the soya sauce and beansprouts. Cook the vegetables for a further minute, then add the rice noodles.

Mix the noodles well into the stir-fry and then serve on a suitable plate. Finally, add the chopped coriander to the vinegar and chilli mixture, and serve a little drizzled on top of the stir-fry and a little on the side.

hearty minestrone with bacon

350 calories

6 g fat

11 g fibre

183 mg calcium, 6 mg iron, 18 mcg selenium, 10 mg beta-carotene, 6 mg vitamin E, 70 mg vitamin C, 119 mcg folate

A good home-made minestrone is a meal in itself and, what is more, this soup can be frozen so you can have plenty made in advance. What is good about minestrone is that you can make it as thick or as liquid as you like, just by adjusting the amount of stock you put in. For vegetarians it is just as good if you omit the bacon.

Low-fat cooking spray
Half an onion, chopped
50 g lean back bacon finely chopped
Pinch dried thyme
Half a leek washed and finely chopped
2 carrots finely chopped
1 clove garlic, crushed
400 g tin chopped tomatoes
1 teaspoon tomato purée
25 g cooked haricot beans (used tinned if you wish)
1 tablespoon tiny pasta pieces or crushed spaghetti

800 ml vegetable stock (use a cube)
Salt and black pepper
Small bunch of fresh basil chopped
1 wholemeal roll to serve with the soup

Place a suitably sized saucepan on the heat and add a little low-fat cooking spray. Once the pan is hot, add the chopped onion and bacon and cook on a moderate heat for 2–3 minutes.

Now add the dried thyme, leek, carrots and garlic and continue to cook for a further 4 minutes, stirring all the time. Once all of the vegetables have softened, add the tinned tomatoes, tomato purée, haricot beans, spaghetti and vegetable stock.

Bring the soup to the boil, turn down the heat and leave to simmer for 20 minutes to bring out all of the flavours. Once the soup is cooked, season with a little salt and pepper and then finish the minestrone by adding the chopped basil leaves.

Serve piping hot with a warm wholemeal roll.

Follow with a 50-calorie Love Bite.

'You Sexy Thing' cottage pie

400 calories

5 g fat

8 g fibre

318 mg calcium, 4 mg iron, 5 mg zinc, 13 mcg selenium, 1 mg vitamin E, 49 mg vitamin C

The classic dishes, such as home-made cottage pie, are real 'comfort food' and, even on this diet you can still enjoy this luxury using our very own tailor-made 'Sexy Thing' pie recipe. We've added a little horseradish to the mash to give it a little bit of zing. Alternatively you could replace beef with lamb and go for the classic shepherd's pie, perhaps also replacing the horseradish with a little Dijon mustard.

200 g of Maris Piper potatoes (available at most supermarkets)

Pan of salted water

Low-fat cooking spray

70 g extra lean minced beef or lamb

Half an onion, peeled and finely chopped

60 g button mushrooms

1 clove garlic, peeled and crushed

Half tablespoon of tomato purée

1 teaspoon plain flour

1 tablespoon tomato ketchup

100 ml beef stock (use a cube)

Salt and pepper
200 ml skimmed milk
1 teaspoon mild horseradish relish or Dijon mustard
salt, pepper and nutmeg
Good-sized portion of peas and carrots to serve aside

Peel and cut the potatoes into small pieces. Place them in a pan of salted water and boil for 12–15 minutes. Meanwhile, heat a non-stick frying pan on a moderate heat with a little low-fat cooking spray.

Add the minced beef and allow the meat to brown slightly. Now add the chopped onion, mushrooms and garlic. Cook until all the vegetables start to soften and then add the tomato purée, flour, ketchup and beef stock.

Let the mixture simmer for 10–12 minutes and season to taste with a little salt and pepper. Meanwhile, once the potatoes are cooked, drain and then return them to the same pan.

Pre-heat the grill to maximum.

Add the milk, horseradish and a touch of salt, pepper and grated nutmeg. Mash the potatoes well until they are fluffy and then leave to one side. Place the meat in a small casserole dish and then spread the mashed potatoes over.

Put the cottage pie under the grill for 6–8 minutes to lightly brown and cook the peas and carrots while you wait. Serve piping hot.

pepper-crusted cod with lime and coriander dressing

300 calories
2 g fat
4 g fibre
99 mg calcium, 5 mg iron,
2 mg zinc, 7 mcg selenium, 1
mg vitamin E, 46 mg vitamin C

This is a simple but effective way of serving cod. You can omit the pepper crust if you are not too keen on the taste of pepper, but it does add an interesting texture and certainly a wonderful flavour to the finished dish. Be sure to get fresh limes and fresh coriander, as the fresh taste of these two ingredients is very important to the finished dish.

1 level dessertspoon whole mixed peppercorns
1 level dessertspoon plain flour, seasoned with a little salt and a pinch paprika
1 150-g portion skinless cod fillet
1 clove garlic, peeled
1 level tsp coarse ground mustard
Grated rind and juice of 1 lime
1 tablespoon fat-free salad dressing
Salt and freshly ground black pepper
Small bunch fresh coriander leaves chopped
Low-fat cooking spray
200 g boiled new potatoes to serve

you sexy thing!

Handful mixed salad leaves to serve

Mix together the crushed peppercorns and seasoned flour.

Remove any bones from the fish and then coat with the peppercorn mixture, pressing well on both sides. Set aside whilst preparing the vinaigrette.

Crush the garlic into a bowl and stir in the mustard, lime rind and juice, fat-free salad dressing, seasoning and coriander.

Heat a non-stick frying pan and add a little low-fat cooking spray. When this is hot, add the fish and fry lightly for 3 minutes on each side, until crisp each side.

Keeping the pan at a moderate heat, pour the vinaigrette around the fish and then turn off the heat. Allow the fish to rest in the dressing for a couple of minutes.

Serve the boiled potatoes hot with the assorted salad leaves on one side. Finally place the fish on the plate and drizzle the lime and coriander dressing around and over the fish.

Add a 100-calorie Love Bite.

love **bites**

For those whose calorie intakes are 1,500 and more per day, you may like to add Love Bites such as a slice of rye bread to a main meal, or have a bowl of soup as a starter to expand a meal. Otherwise, use Love Bites whenever you feel peckish to help keep hunger under control. The slow-release (low-GI) Love

Bites are marked with an asterisk (*). Use these whenever possible. Turn to the other Love Bites only when you really need a treat.

100-calorie love bites

Apples: two *
Banana, medium *
Pear, medium *
Wholemeal toast: 1 slice with Marmite *
Crumpet: 1 toasted with sugar-free jam
Rye bread: 1 slice with peanut butter *
Malt loaf: 1 slice *
Scotch pancake: 1
Borrowdale Teabread: 1 40-g slice
Muesli: 20 g with 100 ml skimmed milk *
Weight Watchers Baked Beans: 175 g *
Minestrone soup, canned: 200 g *
Pea and ham soup, canned: 200 g *
Lentil soup, canned: 200 g *
Tuna in brine, canned: 100 g *
Turkey and chicken slices: 100 g *
Quorn Deli slices: 100 g *
Ice cream: 55-g scoop *
Orchard Maid Raspberry or Strawberry Luxury Frozen Yoghurt: 90-g serving *
Crème caramel: 90 g
Boots Shapers Split yoghurts *
Müller Light yoghurt *
Rice pudding made with skimmed milk: 100 g

St Michael Just Fruit ready-made fruit salad in 160-g pot *

Starburst ice lolly: 1

Jelly: 150 g

Sorbet: 75 g

Boots Shapers New York-style Salted Pretzels

Boots Shapers Crispy Bacon Bites

Boots Shapers Salt and Vinegar Crunchy Sticks

Boots Shapers Indonesian-style Spicy Crackers

Boots Shapers Char-grilled Chicken-flavour Crinkles

Weight Watchers Weavers Smoky Bacon-flavour snacks

St Michael Sundried Tomato and Herb Low-fat Baked Crisps

St Michael Low-Fat French Fries, Salt and Vinegar Flavour

Kallo Chocolate Rice Cakes: 2

Kellogg's Coco Pops Cereal and Milk Bar: 1

McVitie's Go Ahead

    Fig roll: 1

    Digestive biscuit: 1

    Ginger biscuits: 2

    Sponge fingers: 5

    Madeira cake: 1 piece

    Swiss roll: 1 slice

Boots Shapers Turkish Delight Bar: 1

Boots Shapers Mint, Caramel, Coconut, Crispy Caramel or Mint bar: 1

Fruit gums: 60 g

Fruit pastilles: 40 g
Mints: 25 g
Ferrero Rocher chocolate: 1
Fun-size Maltesers, Milky Way, M & Ms, Mars
Halo bar: 1
Milky Way: 1 standard size
Black Magic: 2
After Eights: 3
Match Makers: 5
Quality Street: 2
Lager: 1 x 275-ml bottle
Stout: 1 x 275-ml bottle
Pale ale: 1 x 275-ml bottle
Cider: ½ pint
Wine: 1 glass
Sherry, dry or medium dry: 2 x ⅓ gill
Liqueurs, brandy, whiskey: ⅙ gill

50-calorie love bites

Apricots: 150 g *
Apple: 100 g *
Banana: 1 small *
Blackberries: 200 g *
Cherries: 100 g *
Damsons: 130 g *
Dates: 35 g *
Figs, fresh: 1 *
Grapefruit: 150 g *
Grapes: 90 g *

Guava: 200 g *

Lychees: 100 g *

Mango: 100 g *

Cantaloupe melon: 200 g *

Honeydew melon: 200 g *

Watermelon: 200 g *

Mulberries: 130 g *

Nectarine: 1 *

Oranges: 130 g *

Paw paw: 130 g *

Peach: 140 g *

Pear: 120 g *

Plums: 140 g *

Raspberries: 200 g *

Strawberries 200 g *

Fromage frais, St Ivel Lite 100 g *

Fromage frais, St Michael: 100 g *

Fromage frais, Shape: 100 g *

Fromage frais, Weight Watchers 100 g *

Cadbury's Mini Caramel Egg

Cadbury's Mini Crème Egg

Mini Aero bar

Mini Bounty

Buttermints: 2

Barley sugars: 2

Boiled sweets: 2

use it to lose it:

exercises to keep you **sexy**

Ask most people why they go on a diet and the answer will invariably be 'to lose weight'. Ask them what they mean again and they will probably say something such as 'I want to lose the blubber from my bottom' or 'I want to get rid of the rolls on my stomach.' What they are actually saying, then, is that they go on diets with the intention of losing *fat*.

How devastating, then, to discover that 25% – 30% of the weight lost during those weeks of starvation dieting are not fat at all, but water, muscle, bone and other lean tissue. The faster the weight is lost, the less fat makes up part of it.

So what is the solution? How can you lose weight and maximize the proportion of fat that disappears? The answer is through exercising at the same time as a sensible reduction of total calorie intake. This does not simply mean donning a thong and leaping on to a treadmill. Of course this will burn calories, but strength-training is also vital to ensure fat, rather than muscle and bone, is what is showing as a loss on the scales.

exercise in **action**

Lots of scientific studies have been carried out that prove that cutting down on calories without exercising at the same time leads to loss of muscle and bone as well as fat. Take a look at the results of one study in particular to see what it means in practice.

In a small program, 10 overweight women were given individual food plans that would ensure steady, regular weight loss. Five were asked to undertake strengthening exercises twice a week, the other five were not.

Both groups of women religiously stuck to their eating plans and lost an average of 13 pounds in weight. When their body composition was analysed it was discovered that in those women who had not trained, almost three of these 13 lost pounds was muscle. Those women who had trained gained 1 pound of muscle. This meant that all of the weight lost was fat. In fact, since the new muscle replaced fat, their total fat loss was in fact $14^1/2$ pounds.

exercise and metabolism

As well as helping to improve the definition of the body, maintaining or even slightly adding a little muscle has a crucial affect on your dieting success. By maintaining muscle you also help to maintain your metabolic rate. This means that you are able to even out the body's attempt to slow the metabolism when eating less food.

Anyone who has dieted before will know that what normally happens is his or her metabolic rate drops. This is a cruel yet evolutionarily sensible trick of nature. Not aware whether the lower calorie intake is self-induced or a result of an environmental food shortage, the body slows the rate at which it normally burns energy so that fewer calories are required for survival. So well-tuned is this system that the metabolic rate and thus the number of calories you need to live on can be reduced on drastic low-calorie diets by 30%. A great system if you are in fact starving, and a system that allows people in less fortunate parts of the world to improve their chances of survival. Not such a welcome little number for your body to pull, however, when you are in full control of cutting back on calories and desperate to drop some of that unwanted poundage. This is where the muscle-saving effects of exercise really kick in.

In a nutshell, muscle helps maintain the metabolism. Even when it is apparently doing absolutely nothing more than relaxing, a pound of muscle is burning calories. A pound of fat, on the other hand, simply sits there and burns absolutely no calories at all. Scientists have been able to work out that people who get off their bottoms and start strength-training can improve their metabolic rates by 15%. This can make a lot of difference to achieving your overall weight-loss goals.

This is especially important as we get older, because we lose 5 to 7 pounds of muscle every decade of life. This can decrease our metabolic rate by 2%–5%, which leads to a 15-pound gain in fat every 10 years if we fail to exercise.

The last thing I want is for you to follow a quick-fix diet and end up with a lowered metabolic rate. That is why the delicious meals in the *You Sexy Thing!* meal plan are not set at starvation ration level, and why it is so important to follow Jon's daily exercise plan. Any slight dip in metabolism will be more than made up for by the benefits of increasing muscle activity.

no, you won't look like arnie

And there is no need for women to panic. You will not end up looking like Arnold Schwartzenegger or Sylvester Stallone, nor will you develop the kind of pumped-up biceps that would make Popeye green with envy. Women do not have the right hormonal make-up for this to happen with the kind of plan Jon has put together for you.

For a woman to seriously build muscles you would have to undertake specialist-training sessions, spend hour upon hour in the gym lifting heavy weights, follow special diets and, in some cases, resort to taking illegal steroids.

The *You Sexy Thing!* exercise plan simply aims to improve strength, not build bulk. The exercises will help to stimulate the nerves that supply the muscles. Through springing into action, the nerves in turn will get the muscle fibres to respond and start moving. As this process begins there will be an increase in the production of certain enzymes that use fuel and oxygen, which also helps to improve metabolism.

muscle weighs more than fat

Don't forget, although muscle weighs more than fat it is less bulky. This means that at first you may find that your weight does not seem to be going down that rapidly and yet you look trimmer and slimmer. Since looking good is the main goal, don't panic and start to enjoy your new firmer appearance.

15 days and **then...**

Getting active with Jon's plan is something we really want you to see and feel the benefit of in just 15 days. But, and it is a big but, we also hope that you will be feeling so good after the first two weeks, and that you will be so impressed with the results, that you will keep it up in the long term. Since regular exercise is one of the best ways of helping to stay slim, this surely makes sense. Apart from anything, a good bout of exercise helps release feel-good stress-busting endorphins, and there is evidence that it also tames your appetite.

other benefits

Exercise also improves blood flow, makes the heart and lungs stronger, gives you more flexibility and strengthens bones. Not only that, it helps to stop the declining sense of balance which is another normal part of ageing. With better balance, the risk of falls is reduced and agility and grace noticeably improve. There is no better boost to your self-confidence than knowing that you look graceful as you walk, stand, sit and lie down. Also bear in mind that being sure of your step and having a confident gait are most appealing to others.

There are clearly many benefits from investing time and effort in regular exercise. In addition to balance and grace, improved blood flow can directly enhance your sex life.

blood flow and sex

Blocked arteries, also known as atherosclerosis, is no good for your sex life. It can reduce the amount of blood that gets to the penis, potentially making it more difficult for a man to get and sustain an erection. In women it can reduce the vitality and energy needed for enjoying sex. Raised blood pressure makes the problem even worse.

Exercise, thankfully, has a positive effect on these distressing symptoms. It reduces blood pressure and can lower harmful cholesterol in the blood which leads to and worsens atherosclerosis. It can also improve the condition of blood vessels and local blood flow. Not only that, it helps to stop you gasping for air, which can be a tad embarrassing when trying to impress your intended with an attempt at galloping athletically across the beach or, dare I say it, getting down to fun in the bed chamber.

the stress beater

Exercise is also one of the world's most effective stress-busters. Research confirms that people feel calmer and more relaxed following exercise, and many people report being more able to put things in perspective. Stress is a big problem when it comes to sex. It can extinguish your libido as effectively as a cold shower. Not only that, stress raises bad blood cholesterol levels, increases the risk of blocked-up arteries and has the effect of raising blood pressure. If exercise can directly improve your sex life through helping to get stress under control, it seems like another very good reason to get moving.

nature's night cap

If a lack of sleep is sapping your energy and leaving you more in the mood for sleeping pills than sex, once again, exercise could provide the solution. Not only has exercise been shown to help improve the quality of sleep, research also reveals that it enables people to sleep more deeply, awaken less often in the night and sleep for longer. The equation goes something like this: More exercise = more sleep = more energy for love. What are you waiting for?

more on metabolism –
working yours out

Our metabolism is made up from our resting or basal metabolic rate combined with the increase in metabolism brought about through daily physical movement and exercise. The energy used to maintain our resting metabolism is spent on keeping our heart beating, our lungs breathing and a myriad of other mechanisms, and on the daily repair and growth tasks that the body performs.

The bad news is that resting metabolic rates vary between individuals, just as the colour of our hair and the shapes of our bodies are unique to each of us. Some people inevitably have slightly lower resting metabolic rates, while others have slightly higher ones. This can seem a little unfair if you are one of the slow ones.

The good news, however, is two-fold. The larger you are, the higher your resting metabolic rate. Tests have shown that a woman weighing 16 stone (224 pounds), for example, can have a resting metabolism of 1,900 calories, compared to a 9-stone (126-pound) woman whose resting metabolism is 1,300 calories. As soon as either starts to get active, the number of calories required to maintain weight increases. For the 16-stone woman, a normal lifestyle would burn at least another 800 calories. For the 9-stone woman this would be slightly less.

If you add these figures up, the 16-stone woman has to eat 2,700 calories a day just to maintain her weight, while the 9-stone woman needs more like 2,000. What this means is that if the 16-stone woman reduces her intake to 2,200 calories a day and increases her activity by 500 calories a day, she can lose 2 pounds a week. Her 9-stone companion would need to consume just 1,400 calories a day and increase her exercise by 500 calories a day to achieve the same loss.

estimating your basal metabolic rate (BMR)

1 **If you are between 18 and 30 years of age, multiply your weight in kilograms (1 kg = 2.2 lb) by 14.7. Now add 496 to this figure.**

   If you are between 31 and 60 years of age, multiply your weight in kg by 8.7. Now add 829.

2 **Estimate the number of calories you need for daily activities, as follows:**

   If you mostly sit or stand during the day, multiply the figure you have worked out above by 1.4.

If you do some walking during the day or have quite active hobbies, multiply the figure by 1.7.

If you do a physically active job, multiply the figure by 2.0.

3 Estimate the number of calories you burn during exercise (see list below).

4 Add together the figures from 2 and 3. If you do not do any exercise at the moment, then just use the figure from 2.

Exercise	Calories burned per hour
Running, 6 minutes a mile	1,000
Running, 9 minutes a mile	750
Swimming, fast	630
Squash	615
High-intensity aerobics	520
Swimming, moderate	468
Rowing machine	445
Dancing, fast	444
Tennis, singles	415
Low-intensity aerobics	400
Walking, fast	390
Cycling, 10 miles per hour	385
Badminton	370
Gardening	300
Hiking	270
Cycling, 5 miles per hour	250
Dancing, social	174

To lose around 2 pounds of weight a week, most of which is fat, you need to reduce your calories by 500 a day and increase the number of calories burned by 500 a day to give a total daily calorie deficit of 1,000.

For example, a fairly sedentary 12-stone (168-pound) woman who currently takes no exercise, following the four steps above, would come to a BMR of 2,090. This means that to stay at the same weight she must be getting 2,090 calories a day. If she wants to lose 2 pounds a week, she could cut her caloric intake by 700 calories a day to about 1,400, and undertake some fast dancing, low-intensity aerobics or moderate swimming every day to burn another 300 calories a day.

why it's easier for guys

No one said life was fair, and here is a classic example of the men getting all the luck. A man naturally has around 12% of his body weight made up from fat. A woman has 20%. In a typical man who weighs 73 kg (160 pounds/11 stone 6), there are 64 kg (140 pound/10 stone) of muscle driving his metabolism. In a typical woman weighing 57 kg (126 pounds/9 stone), there is just 46 kg (101 pounds/7 stone 3) of muscle driving her metabolism. This is partly why women need fewer calories than men do.

It is better for us of the fairer sex to get to grips with this fundamental difference between the bodies of guys and girls. This is especially so if we are trying to shape up with our man. Seeing them eating more can make it tempting to dive into larger servings and second helpings ourselves. Remember that we are different and must respect this fact. Doing otherwise will just lead to tears.

age

Also bear in mind that resting metabolic rates decline with age. The resting metabolic rate of an average 60-year-old is 190 calories a day less than that of a person half this age. This is mostly because, from about the age of 40, most women lose a little muscle each year while gaining at least the equivalent amount of body fat. Small amounts of bone are also lost. Around 3 pounds of muscle can be lost in just five years, which has a big effect on the calorie-burning capacity of the body.

There is some good news, though. This natural loss can be compensated for through regularly doing strength-training exercises as discussed. Studies have shown that women over 50 can easily maintain the same resting metabolisms as those in their twenties and early thirties through regular strength-training three times a week.

all extra activity counts

Building in time for Jon's exercise plan is crucial to start to get your body in shape. Maintaining the program will yield fantastic results. Remember, though, formal exercise sessions are not the only way to increase the number of calories you burn each day.

It is surprising how other small changes add up to make big differences over time. The examples that are trotted out in every article you read on weight loss are oldies but goodies. Do try to walk up stairs instead of getting the lift or taking the escalator. Do get out and take a walk every day. Just 15 minutes here and there all adds up.

If you can grab 10 minutes on your own at home, put on some music and have a quick boogie about. Better still, start taking some dancing lessons. Line dancing, salsa, ballroom, whatever appeals. And remember, if you have got to do the housework, use some real elbow grease. Cleaning the windows burns 120 calories an hour, vacuum cleaning 135 and washing the dishes 60. If you have a garden then you had better start digging. Half an hour of that uses up a good 240 calories.

the full **monty**

The *You Sexy Thing!* exercise program is designed to reduce body fat, improve muscle tone, posture and flexibility, reduce stress and increase performance. Not only will you look better, you will feel better and perform better as well.

The only catch is that you will have to follow the

exercise plan strictly over the two-week period to gain these results.

Prior to commencing any exercise program you should always take a health check with your doctor to confirm that you are fit and well to complete the program.

The program is varied and progresses gradually over the two weeks to take you to a level which you should then maintain at a rate of three times a week thereafter. It isolates different qualities of health and fitness and integrates them as you progress and become more proficient.

Above all, the aim of this exercise schedule is to start you along the road to a fitter and healthier lifestyle. If you follow this program to the letter, we promise that you will be very pleasantly surprised by the results!

the calorie-burning component

Aerobic exercise is a great way of burning off the calories. Aerobic exercise is basically any activity which makes you slightly out of breath and increases your heart rate above normal. To get the most out of your aerobic exercise, you should always follow basic guidelines concerning how to warm up and cool down, as well as ensuring that you are not over- (or under!) doing it.

warm-up and cool-down

For the warm-up, complete 5 minutes of light aerobic exercise (i.e. walking or stepping), gradually increasing the pace as the time progresses. Work up to a moderate level of intensity, keeping aware of your posture and technique. This will warm your body up and prepare it for the more vigorous work to follow. You should stretch immediately after your warm-up.

Your cool-down, to be done at the end of the work-out, should last between 3 and 5 minutes and should focus on gradually slowing down your breathing and heart rate. This can be achieved by making the exercise gradually easier every 30 seconds, until you feel once again entirely comfortable. Then stretch to finish.

the rating of perceived exertion (RPE)

In order to optimize the efficiency of your workout, it is necessary to ensure that you are working at the right intensity. As an alternative to a heart rate monitor, the Rating of Perceived Exertion (RPE) scale below gives you a way of judging the level at which you are working. The scale is judged on your own feelings of physical stress, effort and fatigue. You should not focus on any one factor such as shortness of breath, leg pain or exercise intensity, but on your total inner feeling of exertion. In order to ensure that you are working at the right level to gain optimal benefit, you should be at 4 – 7 on the scale of 1 – 10 throughout your aerobic training.

Rating	Description of exercise
0	Nothing at all
0.5	Very, very easy
1	Very easy
2	Easy
3	Moderate
4	Somewhat hard
5	Moderately hard
6	Hard
7	Quite hard
8	Very hard
9	Very, very hard
10	Intensely hard

(Modified from Borg, G. A., *Med. Sci Sports Exerc* 14: 377—87, 1982)

the strengthening and conditioning component

In order to make muscles firm and lean you have to stimulate them by using resistance. The best way is to use your own body weight, and to challenge as many muscle groups as possible in each movement. Completing the resistance exercises will also improve your resting metabolism, aiding in burning off more calories at rest as well as while exercising. The type of training used in this program is of a circuit nature, meaning that you are repeating the exercises with a little rest in between each 'set'. This will stimulate the heart and lungs and add to the calorie-burning value of the workout.

resistance exercises

Start slowly, working on each of these exercises to the point of mild discomfort rather than failure. You should be working towards 10 – 15 repetitions for each exercise, counting to 2 on the upward phase and 2 on the downward phase. This will change as you progress through the program. You should breathe out on exertion and concentrate on keeping perfect form for each repetition. To start you should only attempt one set of each exercise.

squats

Standing with your feet shoulder-width apart, slowly bend at the knees and lower your body until your hamstrings are parallel to the ground. Looking straight ahead and keeping your back in a neutral posture, slowly stand up again.

push-ups

Start by lying flat on the floor with your hands shoulder-width apart, upper arms parallel to the ground. Push up, keeping your body straight, until your elbows are close to full extension. Before the elbows lock, slowly lower and repeat. For a modified version start on your knees instead of toes.

obliques

Lie flat on the floor, bend your knees and place your arms at 90 degrees to your body. From this position, roll onto your left hip and shoulder so that your knees now point diagonally away from you at 45 degrees (rather than to the ceiling). Use the left arm to support your neck, keeping the right arm on the floor. Then slowly reach your left elbow towards your left hip, rotating the body and crunching up, squeezing your ribs towards your pelvis. The right shoulder should not lift off the floor. Repeat on the opposite side.

lunges

Start by taking a split step, making sure that both feet are still pointing forwards. Slowly lunge forward over your front leg, bending the knee. Return to standing, then repeat with the other leg.

dips

From a seated position, keeping the legs slightly bent, edge your backside off the seat so that your arms are holding your body weight. From here, slowly bend the elbows and lower your body until your upper arms are parallel to the ground, pushing up before repeating.

alternate arm/leg raises

Lying flat on your front with your neck lengthened, looking straight down to the ground, slowly lift up your right arm and left leg. Lower and repeat with the left arm and leg.

door pull-ups

Stand with one foot either side of a sturdy door. Hold on to the handles of the door and lean back, keeping the arms straight and legs bent, as if sitting down on an

imaginary chair. Making sure that the feet are firmly anchored, slowly pull forwards until your chest touches the side of the door. Repeat.

step-ups

Use a step that allows for an angle of 45 degrees in your bent knee as you step up onto it. Keep the back straight and step up onto the step, then slowly step back down. Repeat, this time leading with the other leg.

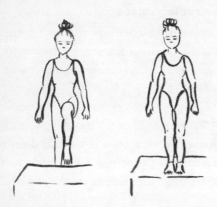

reverse curls

Lie flat on the floor with your knees bent and your arms by your sides. From here slowly lift the feet up and bring the knees into your chest. You are aiming to just elevate your backside off the ground before lowering back down to your start position. It is vitally important that you keep the abdominals tight throughout this exercise – do not relax them on the downward phase.

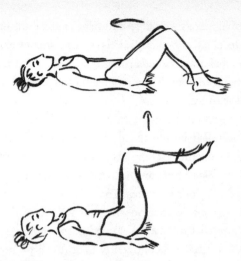

abdominal curls

Lying flat on the ground, bend your knees to reduce the strain on your lower back. From here, supporting your head with your hands, curl forwards to lift your upper back off the ground. Slowly lower and repeat without allowing your head to touch the ground.

the flexibility component

Flexibility is a vital, yet often neglected aspect of fitness. Keeping your body supple will often reduce your risk of injury, as well keep you relaxed and more easily able to carry out everyday tasks. You should always stretch before and after a training session, and it is also beneficial to complete stretches on your rest days to help the muscles to recover.

stretching guidelines

Always take the stretch to a point of mild discomfort and not pain. Ensure that you keep good posture throughout your stretches. To develop a greater range of movement in the muscles you will have to hold each stretch for between 30 and 60 seconds. As you feel the stretch ease off, gently take it a little further until you feel the stretch in the muscle again. Make sure that you never bounce during the movement.

hamstrings

Place your foot onto a chair. Then, keeping your weight-bearing leg slightly bent, slowly fold forwards. Ensure that you keep your body straight and that you bend from the hips, not the waist.

you sexy thing!

quadriceps and hip flexors

Lying on the floor on your side, grasp the ankle of your top leg and pull that leg back behind you to feel the stretch in the front of the leg. Ensure that you keep your knees together and back straight. You should try to bring the knee behind the line of the hip to bring the hip flexors into the stretch.

chest

To stretch the chest and front of the shoulders, place your elbow up against a wall, allowing the upper arm to form an angle of 90 degrees. From here, slowly turn away from the arm that is bent until you feel the stretch in the chest.

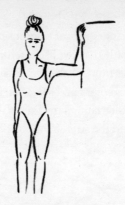

trapezius

Keeping an upright posture, slowly turn your head to one side and then drop the opposite shoulder down to your side to feel the stretch at the side of the neck. Repeat to the other side.

abdominals

Lying flat on your front, rise onto your elbows,

you sexy thing!

bringing the shoulders back and pushing the hips down to feel the stretch in the abdominals.

triceps

Stand upright and bend one arm, placing it behind your head. Pull at this arm (at the elbow) with your other arm to feel the stretch in the back of the bent arm. Repeat to the other side.

shoulders

Standing up straight, pull one arm across the front of your body to feel the stretch in the outside of the shoulder. Make sure that you do not turn as you complete this stretch.

back

Hold onto a fixed object and bend forwards, keeping the knees slightly bent, back flat and arms straight. From here relax the back and tilt the hips from side to side to feel the stretch in either side of the upper back.

the postural component

Holding our body in the correct position is one of the most important factors in maintaining good health. Our skeletons are designed to hold the weight of our body as close to our centre of gravity as possible. The further our skeleton is pulled away from this natural alignment, the higher the incidence of both muscle and joint problems.

In addition to this our posture also sends subconscious signals to those around us. Those who are able to maintain good posture are perceived as more attractive than those who cannot. Changing your posture will change the way that you look at the world as well as the way the world looks at you.

the shoulder squeeze

This exercise draws the shoulders back and lifts the chest.

Stand up straight and slowly rotate the arms out to your sides, squeezing the shoulder blades together and downwards as you go. Hold this position for 10 – 15 seconds before relaxing. Repeat.

neck lift

This brings the head back and into line with the upper spine.

Lie flat on your back on the floor and, keeping the rest of your body still, slowly lift your head up off the floor, just enough so that a sheet of paper could slide underneath. Keep your chin down and your tongue on the roof of your mouth. Hold this position for 10 seconds, relax for 10, then repeat.

lower abdominal compression

This strengthens the lower abdominal muscles and supports the back.

Lie on your back and bend your knees in. Place your hands just under your lower back and then inhale through the tummy, exhale and slowly pull your belly button down and towards your spine. You should aim to gently compress your fingers and maintain this hold for 10 seconds before relaxing for 10 and repeating.

penguin extension

This strengthens the lower back and flattens the curve in the middle back.

Lie flat on your front with your arms down by your sides, palms facing the ceiling. From here slowly lift up from the lower back, rotating the thumbs out and up to the ceiling. Squeeze the shoulder blades together, keeping the head down. Hold in this position for 10 seconds, before relaxing for 10 and repeating.

cat lift

This strengthens the deep abdominals and flattens the lower abdominal region.

Kneel down on all fours, with your wrists directly under your shoulders and your knees under your hips. From here keep your back straight and inhale letting your stomach hang out. From this position exhale trying to pull your stomach in to your spine. Maintain the hold as tight as you can for 10 seconds. Relax for 10 seconds and then repeat.

you sexy thing!

the fifteen-day plan

day one: calorie-burning and postural work

Warm-up and stretch lower body	10 seconds each stretch
Calorie-burning	15 minutes of brisk walking or step-climbing. This should be at an RPE of 3 – 4 to begin with.
Posture	Shoulder squeeze x 5
	Neck lift x 2–3
	Lower abdominal compression x 3
	Penguin extension x 4
	Cat lift x 5
Cool-down and stretch whole body	20 – 30 seconds each stretch

day two: strength and conditioning work

Warm-up and stretch whole body	10 seconds each stretch
Strength and conditioning circuit	Count to 2 on the upward movement and 2 on the downward movement. Complete 1 circuit.
	Squats x 15
	Push-ups x 10
	Obliques x 15
	Lunges x 10 each leg
	Dips x 10

Alternate arm/leg raises
x 10 each side
Door pull-ups x 10
Step-ups x 10 each leg
Reverse curls x 10
Abdominal curls x 10

day three: rest and stretch whole body

Even though this is a rest day, try to increase the
amount of energy you expend on your daily tasks. Try
getting off the bus one stop early and walking a little
further. Use stairs and not the lift, or try to take a short
walk at lunchtime.

Stretching – Complete all the stretches but hold
each one for at least 60 seconds. As you feel the
stretch ease off, slowly increase the stretch. This is
ideally done after a warm bath so that the muscles
are warm.

day four: calorie-burning session

Warm-up and stretch lower body	10 seconds each stretch
Calorie-burning	Complete 20 minutes of brisk walking or step–climbing. This should be at an RPE of 4 – 5.
Cool-down and stretch lower body	20 – 30 seconds each stretch

day five: strength and conditioning and step-climbing interval

Warm-up and stretch whole body	10 seconds each stretch
Step-climbing	3$\frac{1}{2}$ minutes at RPE 4
Strength and conditioning circuit	Count to 2 on the upward movement and 2 on the downward movement. Complete 1 circuit.
	Squats x 15
	Lunges x 12 each side
	Step-ups x 15 each side (Very slow – 3 up/3 down)
Step-climbing	3$\frac{1}{2}$ minutes at RPE 5
	Push ups x 12
	Dips x 15
	Door pull-ups x 15
Step-climbing	3$\frac{1}{2}$ minutes at RPE 6
	Reverse curl x 15
	Obliques x 15 each side
	Abdominal curl x 20
Steady pace walk or step to to finish	10 minutes at RPE 4 – 6
Cool-down and stretch whole body	20 – 30 seconds each stretch

day six: the calorie-burning interval session/postural workout

Warm-up and stretch lower body 10 seconds each stretch

Calorie-burning	Complete one minute of stair-climbing/walking or jogging at an RPE of 6 – 7. Follow this with 2 minutes recovery at an RPE of 4. Repeat this pattern six times, then follow with 7 minutes of steady-pace walking at an RPE of 4 – 5.
Posture	Shoulder squeeze x 7
	Neck lift x 5
	Lower abdominal compression x 5
	Penguin extension x 6
	Cat lift x 7
Cool-down and stretch whole body	20 – 30 seconds each stretch

day seven: rest and stretch

Stretching – Complete all the stretches but hold each one for at least 60 seconds. As you feel the stretch ease off, slowly increase the stretch. This is ideally done after a warm bath so that the muscles are warm.

Ensure that you have a full rest and keep your activity low for the day with the exception of doing the stretching.

day eight: strength and conditioning circuits

Warm-up and stretch whole body	10 seconds each stretch
Strength and conditioning circuit	Count to 3 on the upward movement and 3 on the downward movement. Complete 2 circuits. Take 15 seconds' rest in between the exercises and then 3 to 4 minutes in between each circuit. Squats x 20 Push-ups x 15 Obliques x 17 Lunges x 15 each leg Dips x 15 Alternate arm/leg raises x 15 each side Door pull-ups x 15 Step-ups x 15 each leg Reverse curls x 15 Abdominal curls x 20
Cool-down and stretch whole body	20 – 30 seconds each stretch

day nine: calorie-burning session

Warm-up and stretch lower body	10 seconds each stretch
Calorie-burning	Complete 30 – 35 minutes

	of brisk walking or step-climbing. This should be at an RPE of 5 – 6.
Cool-down and stretch lower body	20 – 30 seconds each stretch. Repeat each stretch twice.

day ten: strength and conditioning and step-climbing interval

Warm-up and stretch whole body	10 seconds each stretch
Step-climbing	4 minutes at RPE 4
	Squats x 20
	Lunges x 15 each side
	Step-ups x 20 each side
	(Very slow – 3 up/3 down)
Step-climbing	4 minutes at RPE 5
	Push-ups x 15
	Dips x 20
	Door pull-ups x 17
Step-climbing	4 minutes at RPE 6
	Reverse curls x 20
	Obliques x 20 each side
	Abdominal curls x 25
Steady-pace walk or step to finish	10 minutes at RPE 5–7
Cool-down and stretch whole body	20 – 30 seconds each stretch

day eleven: postural work and stretch

Warm-up and stretch whole body	10 seconds each stretch
Posture	Shoulder squeeze x 7
	Neck lift x 5
	Lower abdominal compression x 5
	Penguin extension x 6
	Cat lift x 7
Stretching	Complete all the stretches but hold each one for at least 60 seconds. As you feel the stretch ease off, slowly increase the stretch. This is ideally done after a warm bath so that the muscles are warm.

day twelve: calorie-burning workout

Warm-up and stretch lower body	10 seconds each stretch
Calorie-burning	Complete 35 minutes of brisk walking or step-climbing. This should be at an RPE of 5 – 7.
Cool-down and stretch lower body	20 – 30 seconds each stretch. Repeat each stretch twice.

day thirteen: strength and conditioning circuit/calorie-burning session

Warm-up and stretch whole body	10 seconds each stretch
Strength and conditioning circuit	Count to 3 on the upward movement and 3 on the downward one. Complete 2 circuits. Take as little rest as possible in between the exercises, and then 2 to 3 minutes' rest in between each circuit.
	Squats x 25
	Push-ups x 20
	Obliques x 20
	Lunges x 17 each leg
	Dips x 20
	Alternate arm/leg raises x 20 each side
	Door pull-ups x 17
	Step-ups x 17 each leg
	Reverse curls x 20
	Abdominal curls x 25
Cool-down and stretch whole body	20 – 30 seconds each stretch

day fourteen: calorie-burning interval/postural session

Warm-up and stretch whole body	10 seconds each stretch
Calorie-burning	Complete 1 minute of stair–climbing/walking or jogging at an RPE of 6 – 7. Follow this with 1$\frac{1}{2}$ minutes of active recovery at an RPE of 4. Repeat this pattern eight times, and then follow with 10 minutes of steady-pace walking at an RPE of 4 – 5.
Posture	Shoulder squeeze x 9 Neck lift x 7 Lower abdominal compression x 7 Penguin extension x 8 Cat lift x 10
Cool-down and stretch whole body	20 – 30 seconds each stretch

day fifteen: strength and conditioning and step-climbing interval

Warm-up and stretch whole body	10 seconds each stretch
Step-climbing	$4^1/_2$ – 5 minutes at RPE 5
	Squats x 25
	Lunges x 17 each side
	Step-ups x 20 each side
	(Very slow – 4 up/4 down)
Step-climbing	$4^1/_2$ – 5 minutes at RPE 6
	Push-ups x 17
	Dips x 20
	Door pull-ups x 20
Step-climbing	$4^1/_2$ – 5 minutes at RPE 7
	Reverse curls x 25
	Obliques x 25 each side
	Abdominal curls x 30
Steady-pace walk or step to finish	10 minutes at RPE 5 – 7
Cool-down and stretch whole body	20 – 30 seconds each stretch

in the mood:

aphrodisiacs

There are times when even the most ardent of lovers needs a leg up to get their leg over. If Casanova, that celebrated lover of the 18th century, used to feast on oysters to keep up his strength, why shouldn't we? The idea that food and drink can help put you in the mood for romance and spice up your love life is nothing new. Man has been making use of the smell, look or physical properties of food to inspire action in the bedroom for thousands of years.

Classed as aphrodisiacs, these foods and drinks take their name from Aphrodite, the Greek goddess of love. The *Encyclopaedia Britannica* describes an aphrodisiac as 'any food, drink or drug which stimulates sexual desire and power. Popularly, but with slight justification, this property is ascribed to stout, red pepper, oysters, hard-boiled eggs and other foods.'

Indeed, you may well find it difficult to get excited over the thought of a hard-boiled egg, yet for some cultures eggs represent fertility and are quite enough to turn them on. If you think about it, they might think we are a bit odd for thinking that a tub of Haagen Daz ice cream could put us in the mood. Which just goes to show that, to some extent, the effect of an aphrodisiac is all in the mind. It's the association we give to that food that counts. The point must be: if it works, who cares?

Do bear in mind, however, that if you've set your cap at the wrong person, no aphrodisiac is likely to work. If Cupid has aimed his arrow in completely the wrong direction then it's just as likely that your intended will scoff down your carefully selected box of romantic-looking chocolates before saying thanks very much and setting off home. In some cases you might scare a potential date off. I don't recommend, for example, a woman whipping out some ground rhino horn to lace her intended's coffee or waving a phallic-looking ginseng root under his nose hoping for an instant result. Male friends tell me this would undoubtedly have quite the opposite effect.

So when are aphrodisiacs useful? They can certainly be used to fan the embers of a long partnership, helping to lick those old flames of passion into action. There's no doubt that with a bit of careful planning aphrodisiacs may also enhance your chances with someone who has expressed more than a passing interest in taking things a little further.

Do bear in mind that building and maintaining a healthy body is the best way of maintaining a satisfying sex life, helping to keep you physically and mentally in good shape. That said, here are some ideas to help you get in the mood for love. Those I highly recommend I have awarded three stars (***). Some I think sound a bit barmy, but hey, it's a free world. If you fancy giving them a go that's up to you. These get two stars (**). Finally there are others that sound at best uncomfortable and at worst, positively dangerous. They get one star (*).

visual **fantasies**

Foods that look sexy can certainly conjure up all sorts of wild thoughts. It's all down to the Law of Similarities. If a food is reminiscent of an interesting body part, then – given the right circumstances and ambience – it is likely to inspire passion.

asparagus ***

What can I say? You don't need a lesson in physiology to work this one out. Men know that it is essential to watch how a woman approaches these slender stalks. Having dipped the tips in warm butter, does she move them sensuously around her mouth, gently savouring the moment, or does she simply bite their heads off? Apparently this speaks volumes about potential future antics. Having given a girl the 'Asparagus Test', you men out there may want to call the whole thing off before you get to the main course!

oysters ***

Frequently perceived as the ultimate aphrodisiac, take a glance at an oyster lying lasciviously open on its half shell and it's not hard to see why Don Juan simply couldn't get enough of these treats from Neptune's larder. Actually his passion for them might not simply have been their looks and the succulent, moist affair of swallowing them whole, but may also have had something to do with their nutritional content. Oysters are in fact the richest source of zinc in the diet, a mineral which if lacking in men leads to impotence. Thankfully this particular cause of impotence is completely reversible on the restoration of this essential nutrient.

bananas ***

Someone once told me that French mothers teach their daughters not only the sartorial tricks of the trade to ease their passage to womanhood – how to choose perfume, coiffure their hair, select stylish clothes and so on – but they also give advice on the art of eating bananas erotically. There is little doubt that female 'chompers' demonstrate a decidedly scary approach when tackling this fruit, which may subconsciously frighten the life out of a potential male suitor. Taking things gently, perhaps breaking small pieces off before eating them, is a more delicate and less intimidating method of consumption. Men, on the other hand, should just get on with the business of downing bananas, doing so with a robust and masterful vigour. That's very sexy.

figs ***

Slice open a fresh fig and there you see its soft pink colour and lines of little seeds that ripple gently inwards from the edges to meet in the middle groove. In some parts of the world, so exotic is the sight of this succulent, moist fruit that it gives its name to a female's private parts. Serve figs 'nude' (peeled) on romantic picnics; drench with runny, clear honey to end a romantic dinner or with a little creamy yoghurt for a special breakfast in bed. Take in the beauty of this fruit and transport yourself back to those decadent, indulgent Roman feasts where figs were a centrepiece.

honey ***

Dripping, golden, warm; this nectar of the gods has been linked to love since time began. Even today newlyweds slink away to consummate their marriage on 'honeymoon', while way back in the 5th century BC the Greek physician Hippocrates was prescribing this delicious labour of the bees for sexual vigour. Share this heavenly delight straight from the spoon, pour languidly over baked fruits or lick it from your lover's fingers. Ummm ...

avocado pear ***

When peeled, there is little doubt that this silken, smooth fruit resembles so much the decadent female curves of screen goddesses past. A delight to the touch, close your eyes and conjure thoughts of the very softest of skins.

grapes ***

Orgiastic feasts, decadence and the unadulterated pursuit of pleasure. That's what grapes are made of. The ultimate 'feed each other' food. Lie back with a bunch of succulent, seedless, sweet, juicy grapes and let your imagination run riot. I guarantee you won't finish the bunch.

cherries **

Similarly synonymous with sex, cherries, like grapes, are made for couples to feed each other. Disposing of the stones makes them slightly less alluring, although the blushed red of the flesh and skin can be tantalizing in their ability to evoke a sense of innocence.

ginseng **

Have you seen the root of the ginseng plant? Bearing an uncanny resemblance to a certain part of the male anatomy, the amatory properties of ginseng go way beyond its masculine form.

stimulating **smells**

Women's olfactory senses are said to be one thousand times more sensitive than men's, but that doesn't mean men can't be tempted...

strawberries ***

The scent of a strawberry is said to stimulate blood flow in men to all the crucial regions. Combine this with strawberries' naturally romantic and luxurious connotations and you have the recipe for love.

mushrooms **

Sixteenth-century French noblemen were said to go wild for mushrooms, believing their smell to resemble the intoxicating notes of a lover's bed.

truffles **

Madame de Pompadour was a sucker for truffles. She loved nothing more than the 'Canal notes' of their musk-like odour. An exorbitant and extravagant way of enticing your woman, the treat of the truffle lies also in the 'Rule of Rarity' – like investing in an expensive dinner, only you can decide if she's worth it.

coriander **

The seeds of the coriander plant release scents to send you swooning into thoughts of sensual

Oriental pleasures. Slightly sweet and reminiscent of enchanted orange groves, indulge in a creamy, coriander-rich curry to heighten the senses for your 'second course'.

cinnamon **

Once so rare and prized, cinnamon's heady scent fills your head with its rich aroma. Whether it's through a warming glass of mulled wine, a cinnamon and apple tea or a special cinnamon-flavoured sweetmeat, float away on this spice of love deep in thoughts of the erotic East.

the taste and feel of **love**

Favourite tastes are favourite tastes. No one can tell you what you should prefer and what should turn you on. There is little doubt, however, that some foods and drinks have an almost universal ability to get the mouth watering and press those vital buttons.

chocolate ***

No other substance shares the exquisite property of melting at body temperature; hence the luxurious feel as chocolate quite literally dissolves in the mouth. It's also a positive cocktail of amatory experiences just waiting to unleash themselves as they touch the tongue. Take its ability to stimulate the release of feel-good endorphins, its phenylethy-lamine – said to be the substance we release in our brains when in love – and the little kick of caffeine it supplies to perk up our systems. Add to this the controlled boost to our blood sugar levels and it's no wonder it's described as the food of the Gods.

champagne ***

A symbol of sheer indulgence, the sensation of gentle bubbles slipping down the throat exhilarates and titillates palate, mind and soul. Pink champagne is said to be the most romantic drink in the world. Sip slowly from shallow coupe glass, modelled on the breasts of Marie Antoinette, or from a long, elegant Audrey Hepburn-style flute; either way, make sure it's cold for the full effervescent experience.

mango ***

Feed each other with slithers of this exotic, fragrant fruit. Feel the silken flesh as it slips through your fingers and you catch the juices on your tongues.

ice cream ***

Sharing a pot of ice cream (and obviously the spoon) is considered by some to be the ultimate turn-on and is just one step away from a good ravaging. Lick it, suck it and swirl it around your mouth, advises psychologist Dr Sidney Crown.

tricks of the **trade**

Frankly, the rest of these get just one star. Some even rate only a star minus (*-). I'd strongly advise you *not* to try them, even in the privacy of your own home, but forewarned is forearmed and if an over-excited lover tries one of these on, you will at least be armed with some good reasons to extricate your-self from the experience.

chillies *-

According to ancient texts, Arab men ground up chillies and applied them to their private parts to get their juices, and blood, surging. Quite how this affected their women folk one hardly dares consider!

white thorn apple *-

Not satisfied with chillies, in times long past Asian gents were known to rub a mix of ground white thorn apple mixed with honey to their bits in the hopes that women folk would succumb to its seda-tive properties, relinquishing all guile and giving in to their man's dearest desires. I don't think so.

chrysocalla *-

Back to the Near East long, long ago, guys were vain enough and daft enough to eat Chrysocalla, better known as borax, to achieve a very impressive

firmness. Apparently, and I quote, it was used for '...
Increasing the dimension of small members and for
making them splendid'. Let's not get too disparag-
ing. I'm sure one day, way in the future, there could
be people giggling over our use of Viagra.

stallion genitalia *

I kid you not. Chinese men would cook them up and
down them in one. With this plus the tinkering bells
they would attach to their bits, the women folk
must have been in seventh heaven.

the science of **aphrodisiacs**

In some instances ancient aphrodisiacs have, at least
in theory, a scientific rationale as to why they may
just work.

garlic ***

While mediaeval herbalists in England wittered on
about garlic's ability to cleanse the blood, tone
organs and generally build up stamina, it's real con-
tribution to a good sex life probably comes from its
proven ability to reduce the fatty build-ups on artery
walls, which in turn increases blood flow. These fatty build-ups don't just occur around the heart and
lead to heart disease, they can occur in the big blood
vessels 'down there' – and you can imagine the

problems *that* causes. Less blood flow means less of an erection. Not only this, women may benefit from extra blood to their nether regions. So it's garlic all round.

oysters ***

There's definitely more to oysters than their suggestive 'come hither' looks. They are packed with the mineral zinc, and we know for sure that a lack of zinc leads to impotence. Restore levels and it's up, up and away. Just one oyster supplies 5 mg of this wonder nutrient. Men need around 10 mg daily.

muira puama **

This wonder herb, whose name when translated means 'potency wood', is the colloquial name given to the Brazilian shrub *Ptychopetalum olacoides*. For many centuries the Amazonian Indians have supplemented their diet with Muira puama, a dynamo to their sexual appetite. Recent research conducted at the Institute of Biosexology in Paris has shown it to improve circulation and have beneficial effects on human sexuality.

Muira puama is available as Herbal v-Y for men and Herbal v-X for women from health food stores.

ginkgo biloba ***

Used to improve circulation, some nutritionists swear by this supplement for improving their patients' sex lives. In men it is said to help improve blood flow to the penis and thus be a treatment for erection problems caused by inadequate blood flow.

dong quai ***

Often used to help menopausal symptoms such as vaginal dryness and a flagging libido, dong quai has been used in Asia for centuries. Taking 500-mg capsules three times daily could be helpful for women.

st john's wort ***

Trials on menopausal women with the Kira brand of this herb have been shown to improve sex drive. One-a-day tablets of Kira are available from health food stores and chemists.

ginseng **

According to some researchers, the wild Manchurian variety of ginseng found in China has a particularly stimulating effect on the endocrine glands and thus increases testosterone production – just what's needed to help rejuvenate a flagging libido. Older Chinese men who've been taking it for years would back up such claims. Scientists also say it contains steroidal saponins which make the body more responsive to the hormone adrenaline, giving the illusion of improved performance. Work carried out on some lucky mice found that ginseng not only increased the size of their gonads, but their rates of copulation too. Other animal studies have shown that ginseng increases testosterone levels and sperm production. No such spectacular results have been proven in humans, but if you fancy giving it a go, you can find it in all good health food stores, in capsules or in a powdered form to add to your tea.

astralagus **
Used in China as a tonic for revitalizing and restoring sexual energy in men and women, three 400-mg capsules a day can be taken.

yohimbe *
Another gem from a far-off continent, this time America. Available only on prescription, Yohimbe is obtained from the bark of a tree and apparently stimulates sexual desire and improves potency in about half of the men who give it a whirl. The other 50% get very anxious on it. Yohimbe can increase blood pressure and should only be taken under supervision of your doctor.

nice try ... but i don't think **so!**

carrots and parsnips
Maybe they were once considered to be sexy, but nowadays they don't make it on to the clapometer for revving up one's sex life.

coconuts

Same goes for coconuts. Hairy and hard they may be, but their ability to inspire lust in contemporary couples must surely be doubted.

spanish fly

This 'love powder' made from the dried and powdered remains of a beetle found in southern Europe may have been used since Roman times to stimulate the sexual appetite of the Emperor Tiberius, but it is rather dangerous and best avoided – even if you can find anyone selling the stuff.

rhino horn

Another ancient aphrodisiac which is not worth the cost even if you could get hold of some. Fabled as a potent aphrodisiac, sadly its actions are just that – a fable.

the cut of your jib:

tips on clothing, posture, skincare and
more to make **all the difference**

If, after all the effort of following the *You Sexy Thing*
eating and exercise program you feel in need of an
extra boost of confidence, then dive into this chapter
and earn yourself the first-ever degree in cutting cor-
ners to looking good. Models do it, for goodness' sake,
so why shouldn't we?

It is incredible how spending a bit of time on
pampering your skin, correcting your posture,
choosing the right cut of clothes or swimming costume and avoiding certain foods and drinks can
make the world of difference to how you look and,
most importantly, how you *feel* about yourself.

In search of the best person around to kick-start
the process, I asked Janet Menzies, author of *Cheat at
Slimming*, to share some of her top tips with us. Janet
worked as Woman's editor on the *Daily Express* as
well as on *Hello!* and the *Daily Mail*. She knows a
thing or two about how the rich and famous milk the
tricks of the trade to create those perfect shimmering
images that appear in the magazines, newspapers and

on television and movie screens across the world.

The first thing that I learned from Janet is that there is more to that old saying 'keeping up appearances' than first meets the eye. As Janet explains:

What most people want is to appear to look good. There are many ways to achieve that goal that don't involve anything to do with eating. For example, the truth is that knickers are what cause a VPL (visible panty line), not flesh; it's peroxide, not dieting, that makes you blonde; and high heels, not self-denial, are what makes you taller. So if you want to be tall, buy stilettos; if you hate your mousy hair, go to the hairdresser's; and if you've got a VPL, take your knickers off.

Wow, there you have it. So, one of the main things you need to do when working out how to improve on your current appearance is to be clear exactly what it is that you want to achieve. Once that is done, you need a game plan for putting it into action. Feeling that you have improved your appearance will do wonders for your self-confidence and, at the end of the day, that, as much as anything, is what's going to make you feel sexy.

There are three areas to concentrate on that can give particularly quick results: 'optical illusions', posture, and skincare.

optical **illusions**

The cut of your costume, the shape of those bikini bottoms, the length of your dress or the tailoring of your trousers – everyone, men and women, can learn the art of optical illusion to make big bits look smaller and small bits look bigger, and make the very most of your figure.

on the beach and by the pool
women

I'll let Janet explain:

High-cut legs on bikinis and swimming costumes help to lengthen and slim the thighs. High-waisted, lower leg 'tap pants' diminish the stomach and bottom. Broad straps make the arms look thinner and a v-shaped front makes the bust look neater. When it comes to spots ... If it's polka dots you are into, then have big ones if you are tall and heavy-framed; little ones if you are short. Vertical and diagonal stripes as well as 'panels' help minimize the stomach. With bold patterns, usually the rule is the fewer the better, so try to avoid large floral designs where possible. Deep colours tend to look good (leave the day-glo yellows and oranges for the teenagers) and try to go for matt, not shiny fabrics.

Typical pear-shaped women are better off drawing

the adoring gazes of potential admirers away from the hips. This can be done not only with high-legged bikini bottoms, but also by having plain colours in a swimming costume around the hips and bottom, and having a lighter colour at the top. If you have a small bust, then go for costumes with jazzier tops, with gathers or some kind of bow. Skirted costumes are a real no-no, but then you probably knew that.

If you are lucky enough to have a good bosom, then my advice is to flaunt it. If you think it is too big and would rather be less obvious about display-ing your assets, then a costume with little detail around the bust is the best option. Extra frills just make it more obvious.

men

Men are advised to avoid those little skimpy briefs when it comes to their beach attire. Even Mark Spits would have looked ridiculous scampering around on his holidays in a pair of tight 'Speedos'. If you have any tummy or bottom at all, they are a complete disaster. The boxer short-style swimming trunks are much more flattering and hide a multitude of sins, although do take a bit of time to get the length of the leg right. The ones that go practically down to the knees can make you look short and leave you resembling a cross between a Boy Scout and a jungle explorer.

undies

When it comes to day and eveningwear, good fitting undies are crucial for men and women alike. There is no benefit in having what you think is the sexiest, briefest gear on underneath, if the effect displayed to the outside world is less than flattering. You might never get to the bedroom.

bras

When it comes to bras it really is worth getting a good fitting in a store which has properly trained staff. You need the correct back size and the correct cup size. New bras should be able to fit when done up on the middle hook. If you are doing yours up on the loosest or tightest set of hooks, you need a new one. This is true too if your current bras ride up at the back or if your bosom is bulging over the top or sides of your cup.

knickers

On the knickers front, don't be tempted by a thong if it doesn't feel right. G-strings and cami-knickers often look better on the hangers than they do once you've pulled them on. What can be less comfortable than knickers riding up your bottom or bits squidging out all over the place?

If you aren't tempted to go 'knickerless' to avoid a VPL, then make sure you get the right size briefs. Don't be completely taken in by pants with built-in 'control' panels. They may help tame slightly bulging tummies but if they are too controlling, they usually just end up pushing the untoned bits off in another direction.

tights and stockings

Of course stockings are the sexiest option. If you feel comfortable in them, then that's great. For the rest of us, there are Lycra tights. As Janet says:

The invention of Lycra has turned hosiery into a dieter's secret weapon. Most people have discovered the virtues of opaque matt black heavyweight tights for daywear, but there are subtler ways of achieving a thigh-slimming, leg-lengthening effect.

For achieving this result Janet recommends the sheer look, telling me that it's actually more flattering than opaque, and makes a less obvious cover-up. Janet warns:

Gloss hosiery should be avoided. Matt black tights look best on tall people. Most flattering colours for people of every size are dark neutral, pewter grey, dark brown and nearly black. Tan, pale, white and pastels should be avoided.

If it's a summer's evening and your legs haven't quite got that sun-kissed look, go for the sheerest type possible that is just slightly darker than your normal colour. A 10 to 15 denier uses a fine yarn and gives a good result. One point, though – don't show off the reinforced toe piece with sandals. If a guy notices, it will be a sure turn-off.

top tights tips

- **If tights tend to dry your legs out, leaving flaky bits of skin falling to the floor as you remove them, try the Pretty Polly range of moisturizing tights that release moisturizer into the legs throughout the day. They last up to five washes.**
- **'For dramatic effect,' says Janet, 'borrow the fashion editors' trick of wearing a pair of fishnets over a fake tan in summer or over dark skin-tone tights in winter.'**
- **Control-top tights can help to flatten the stomach – but never be tempted to buy a smaller size for extra control. Your stomach has to go somewhere and will simply travel up and over your waistband.**

pants

Guys, always make sure that your pants fit. Tight boxer shorts or briefs are really not on. Blubbery bits are less likely to splurge over the top if they are not too tight.

Also, a word of advice. Forget boxer shorts with seasonal decorations like Santa Claus. Disney characters are fine if you are seven, but are not sexy. Nylon undies are a complete no-no. If you like white cotton Calvin Klein styles with buttons up the front, that's great; a lot of girls find them very sexy. Whichever style you go for, make sure they are WHITE. Over-washed 'grey' versions are a turn-off. Good value options can be found at Gap as well as good old M & S.

clothes you don't need to die of embarrassment for

thigh problems

Is there a woman in the world satisfied with the way she looks? I doubt it. There is always something we want to change, and thighs seem to come pretty high up on the list of most-loathed area.

skirts and dresses

For the majority of pear-shaped figures, thighs can look heavy. Certain clothes can make this 10 times worse. Janet explained to me how optical illusions can help disguise thighs:

The most important visual tactic for big thighs is getting the length right for dresses and skirts, and it is a trick that most of us get wrong.

Apparently, in our anxiety to reveal the slimmer bits of the leg, the common mistake is to choose a hemline that stops exactly where the fat part of the thigh begins. 'When the eye cannot see something it supplies an imaginary picture, based on an extension of what it can see.' This, says Janet, means that if a hemline stops where the widest part of the thigh begins, the eye recognizes the concealed part of the leg as also being thick.

If the hemline is dropped slightly so that it falls in the middle of the narrowest part of the leg, the eye assumes that the rest of the leg is equally narrow – and by magic you appear to have thinner legs.

The trick, therefore, is to get all three hemline areas (thigh, knee and calf/ankle) correct.

- **Thigh hemline: If your thigh is narrowest just above the knee, then show your whole knee. This suggests that this narrow above-knee area continues all the way up.**
- **Knee hemline: If your thighs are thick all the way down, then the hemline should rest in the middle of the knee.**
- **Calf/ankle hemline: 2.5 cm above the ankle bone is a flattering hemline because the eye focuses on the narrowness of the Achilles tendon, especially when high heels are worn.**

Don't rule out mini-skirts however because you think you have big thighs. The correctly shaped mini-skirt, teamed with the right hosiery, can do wonders for even the most thunderous thighs.

The best shape to go for is what Janet calls the lampshade shape, which rests loosely on or just above the hips and flares out in an A-line. Tulip-shaped skirts of any length are a disaster, minis included, because they follow the line of the bulge and then cut into the thighs.

If you are not quite sure which length will make the most of your legs, then fashion experts recommend putting on your tights and shoes and standing in front of a mirror with a towel. Use the towel as an imaginary skirt, adjusting the length as if it is a skirt to establish the most flattering length for you.

Once you get to know which hemline lengths suit you for above and below the knee, do not be tempted to make rash purchases of clothes that don't fit the bill, however charming they look on the hanger in the shop. It is also a good idea to keep an eye out for dresses with a V-shaped bodice, as these help to 'lengthen' the thigh by drawing the eye upwards.

trousers

When it comes to trousers, getting the cut right is vital. They can be an extremely effective way of slimming down the look of the leg. Janet explained to me:

Trousers help to lengthen the look of your legs if you conceal high heels underneath. If you do not feel comfortable teetering around on heels, you can find a pair of shoes with slightly stacked heels and sole, which when teamed with a slight flare or 'boot-leg' balances the width of your upper leg.

Cruise-cut trousers which widen gradually right from the hipbones downwards are a clever way of smoothing the overall profile into a steady, straight line rather than a bulging one. A pair with some form of detail on the outside seam, such as extra stitching, braiding or a stripe, can take inches off the appearance of the thighs, because the eye stops where the block colour stops and the detail starts.

big bottoms
skirts and dresses

To take the emphasis away from the bottom it is necessary to enhance the bustline. This can be achieved through good tailoring and wearing the right kind of good-fitting bra. It also helps to wear some kind of shoulder padding. This makes the shoulders, rather than the bottom, the widest part of the body.

As far as skirts go, the advice from Janet is to go for those that drape softly rather than ones that cling to the figure. Wrap-arounds in flowing fabrics are apparently the best type for this. Again, tulip skirts should be avoided because they just make the bottom look bigger. Gathered skirts are also out. Box pleats are a better choice, helping to draw the eye inwards, away from bulges.

One of the cardinal sins committed by those trying to disguise their bottom is having the waistline too tight. There is a tendency to think that if you have at least got a small waist, you may as well make the most of it. Sadly, all this does is to make people look even more closely at the disparity between the two body parts.

Janet suggests a longer line look. 'This can be created by wearing a straight, ribby sweater that ends just below the hips, or echo this shape with a tunic top.'

Another of her tips is to choose shirt-style dress-es, which give you the option of moving the belt to the most flattering position.

trousers

While these can be a saving grace to girls with big thighs, bottoms that are on the large side can suffer ter-ribly in trousers. Janet advises:

Men's jeans worn a size too big and slightly clinched in with a cowboy belt can help the bottom dis-appear as well as looking hip and chic. Well-cut dark cigar pants with the zip in the side or up the middle of the bottom help to magically neaten the silhouette and can be dressed up or down for evening and day wear.

clever use of colour

This is also an important tool in the box of tricks when it comes to disguising bottoms. As Janet says,

Forget black skirts and white tops. The eye is irre-sistibly drawn by the contrast between the black of the skirt and the white of the shirt above. Everyone forgets that black can highlight just as easily as it can conceal.

Instead, Janet says the best way to draw the eye away to better features is to make the bottom part a gradual gradation of colour. It doesn't even matter whether it is darker or lighter than what is above, it just mustn't contrast.

If you need to be formal, try wearing a hip-length black jacket with a charcoal-grey skirt and neutral tights. For a more dynamic look, team a ribby jumper in rust with a long claret-coloured wrap-around skirt and high heels.

waist

Ever felt like your stomach is walking into a room before the rest of you? Ever felt like your waistband is about to pop open and liberate all the flesh it's struggling to hold back? Thick waists are indeed a problem area. But take heart, sticky-out stomachs are the easiest of all the different hot spots to improve on.

Choosing firm fabrics is a must. Gabardine and flannel will not tend to sag or stretch. Shiny, stretchy fabrics create real difficulties and should be avoided, since they crease and gather around the bulging tummy.

Buying the right size is also crucial to the camouflage. Tight skirts and dresses just emphasize the potbelly look. A side-zipped skirt or a well-cut pair of trousers allow for a broad, flat central panel that helps to flatten the tummy.

Belts are also invaluable, especially for those with short waists. The illusion of length is given by using a belt to define the area where you would like your waist to be. Slung loosely round the hips, a belt helps to provide the eye with a visual break. If you have an hourglass figure, the belt that fits neatly stops the curves running together.

busts

Janet Menzies is clear on the necessary course of action for small busts:

Forget all the rules. Go wild and shiny and make the most of tight stretchy materials, all of which give the illusion of curves. Padded and wired bras are an obvious choice, but have you ever thought of the trick used by the stars to try a cup size too small so that almost whatever your natural size, something spills out over the top?

The other useful hint from Janet was gleaned from her make-up artist friends:

Their trick, which is useful for evenings, is to dust the cleft of what little cleavage you have with a little shiny bronzing powder, giving the impression of a deeper shadow than really exists.

If on the other hand you are trying to make your bust appear smaller, the key is to try giving a good 'V-line' shape to the area. This can be achieved through wearing a V-neck jumper, or V-neck jackets and shirts with the collar open. As Janet points out:

This V-shape can be further emphasized through wearing

a scarf with the knot just tied just between the breasts or wearing a long pendant that lies in the same place. Fussy necklines, lots of detailed patterns or stitching round the chest should be avoided, as should yoke-style necks, gathers and pleats. These simply bolster the breasts and give the opposite effect to that intended.

men

on the short side

Double-breasted suits are not a good option. Instead, go for single-breasted jackets and suits without turn-up trousers. As a rule, men under 5'7" should avoid turn-ups. Try to buy vertical lines such as pinstripes and remember that all-in-one colour produces an elongating effect. Fitted styles of all clothes, whether smart or casual, are better than the baggy look, which simply shortens the legs further.

tall men

If you feel that you would like to appear less lanky, then breaking the line between your trousers and your top half by wearing different colours top and bottom helps. When it comes to suits, then you need to go for turn-ups.

wide guys

As for shorter men, single-breasted suits are best teamed up with pale-coloured shirts. Shirts and suits with contrasting buttons can help draw the eye away from your width, but do not be tempted by narrow belts and waistcoats. Blouson jackets and elasticated waists are also out. Sadly those winter woollies could well need a turn-out too. Thick knits will just make you look even chunkier.

beer bellies

Anything stretched over the stomach will make it appear bigger, so throw out all of those tight T-shirts, shirts and jumpers. You never see Pavarotti in a clingy little number; he's big, but he's also Italian and knows how to dress for his size. The other disaster zone is, of course, the trouser area. The 'builder's bottom' has never – and never will be – 'in'. Buy trousers that fit. With suits, make sure they are well cut. Dark-coloured jackets tend to give the impression of broader shoulders and help to stop the eyes falling girthwards. Braces can be good for those with stomachs bigger than they would like.

Remember some basic rules, whatever your shape and size:

- With trousers, always be able to insert two fingers widthways into the waistband. If you cannot do this, they are too tight.
- Pleats on trousers should hang easily and drape. If they gape, the trousers are too small for you.
- If trousers have belt loops, then a belt should be worn. If braces are chosen instead, remove the belt loops.

- With jackets, also be sure that the vents lie flat. A stretched vent means you need a bigger size.
- Make sure that your tie finishes at your waistband. If it finishes above the waist, you risk looking like you are about to head off to school; if below, it ruins the proportion of the outfit.

posture

We've all seen those famous 'before' and 'after' photographs showing people standing with their shoulders hunched over, their tummies and bottoms poking out and with a pretty down-in-the-mouth expression on their faces. Then, hey presto, there's the second shot: standing tall, shoulders back, stomachs all but disappeared and bottoms tucked up and under. More often than not, the 'after' has a lot to do with a change in posture and far less to do with any miracle lotion or potion advertised alongside.

To check out your own posture, Janet Menzies suggests standing in front of a mirror and taking a long, hard look at yourself. The aim is to give up the 'sack of potatoes' look, replacing it instead with the pose and stance of a supermodel.

Changing your figure by improving your posture is actually one of the oldest tricks in the book. It works well enough to sell thousands of home-toning machines every year. Flick the pages in any colour supplement and you'll see adverts showing men and women miraculously transformed from pot-bellied, sway-backed, droopy-busted, round-shouldered tubbies into gazelle-like creatures.

Janet suggests this seven-point plan:

1 **Turn sideways to the mirror and let yourself droop. Release all the muscles in your abdomen and let your stomach protrude as far as it wants – let it go even further by collapsing your spine and dropping your shoulders. For added effect, slouch your head down. Now concentrate on your shoulder blades. Move the flat blades across your back towards the spine, pulling them downwards as you do so. You will notice immediately that you have to open out the points of your shoulders and raise your chest.**

2 **As your shoulder blades arrive in their new position, take the opportunity to raise your chest still further. Do this by imagining a string attached to your sternum, the point where your ribs meet, and pulling upwards to so that your chest lifts.**

3 **When your chest lifts you will find you automatically raise your chin and lengthen your neck.**

4 **Now take a deep breath in, allowing your whole ribcage to lift and widen in order to accommodate the breath.**

5 **When it comes to expelling the breath, use the**

muscles in your slack abdomen to do it. **Tighten those muscles in order to press the air out from the bottom – as though you were squeezing toothpaste out of a tube. Keep the ribs in the flared-out position as you do so.**

6 Once you have breathed out the air, relax your tummy muscles only slightly so that they remain taut and pulled in, but comfortably so.

7 By now the swayback of the 'before' picture will have almost gone, along with the tummy and rounded shoulders. To add the finishing touches, stretch your whole spine upwards and tuck your buttocks in.

It is important to take time to get used this new you, and it requires practice. Exercises can help to develop muscles that make this posture easier to hold. Pilates is particularly good for developing good posture – or 'body alignment', as Pilates expert Lynn Robinson calls it:

The body is a closed system. If one part of it is out of alignment, then the whole structure is altered. The good news is that bad alignment can be corrected with a Pilates conditioning program.

Crucial to good posture is the development of what Joseph Pilates, founder of this method, called a 'girdle of strength'. The girdle is created by strengthening the muscles that support your spine and internal organs. These form a criss-crossing effect in the torso. 'These help to create a strong, firm stomach,' says Lynn.

skincare

a tanned skin looks slimmer

Everyone knows that too much sun damages the skin. But we also know that all those people who've been on the beach *appear* healthier and, let's admit it, slimmer.

Yes, a tan makes you look thinner. Obviously this makes changing the colour of your skin one of the quickest cheats in the book. Janet Menzies counsels:

Pale white skin reflects more light than browner skin, and a shiny surface, whether on dark- or light-skinned people, also reflects additional light off the curves of the body. The more light that is reflected, the more the body's bulges are accentuated, and the bigger the overall impression of the body.

This means a tanned, matt-skinned person will look slimmer than someone with pallid, shiny skin. Applying fake tan is therefore a must in your Emergency Rescue Plan.

If the idea of fake tan fills you with horror, leaving images of stripy legs and over-bronzed unrealistic tans, rest assured, the fake tan market has moved on from those disastrous products of the early days.

Absolutely crucial to a good fake tan result is making sure that you exfoliate your skin first to avoid extra tan soaking into dry and rough bits, for example on the elbows and knees. This can either be done with a special exfoliation cream or by using a skin brush or a mitt designed especially for the job.

When it comes to the tan itself, there are lots on the market. One of the best products that will do the job without breaking the bank is *St Tropez Fake Tan*. Apparently it is the fake tan they use on the set of Melrose Place, where the ever-tanned guys and gals lounge around the pool all day. At around £30 for a top-to-toe tan in a professional salon, it's worth the money. If you want to go DIY, then they do the *St Tropez Auto Bronzant* tanning lotion that costs half the price for 100 mg. This creamy lotion is tinted so you can see where you're putting it.

Good beauty brands such as Estée Lauder, Clarins and Le Roc also do very good versions of fake tans. All come with clear instructions and a list of Dos and Don'ts regarding the exact method of application and how many times you need to top it up for the honey-kissed look.

When considering a self-tan, remember to leave yourself plenty of time. It takes a while to apply and then dry. Trying to rush things will usually backfire.

broken veins

Packing your diet with berries rich in antioxidants, which help strengthen the microcirculation, is thought to be a wise way of reducing the risk of future broken veins. This does not help with the broken veins you already have, though, of course. If fake tan is not enough to cover up areas of vein damage, you could think about sclerotherapy. This salon treatment is based on injecting a special sclerosing solution into the dead vein. It helps the body to heal and in effect removes the dead vein from show. Half-hour sessions are carried out by trained practitioners and need to be repeated three to four times for really good results. Check with your local beauty salons to see if they offer this service.

sexy legs

What wouldn't you do for Julia Roberts-style legs? Long, lean, slim, up to her armpits and out-and-out sexy. Of course it would be nice to have legs with such fabulous vital statistics. Most of all, it would be nice to have legs so smooth and dimple-free. You won't see the barest smidgen of the dreaded 'C' word on her perfect pins.

Of course no one could dream of writing a book on looking sexy for the beach and bedroom without addressing the perennial problem and plague of many a woman's life: CELLULITE. That lumpy old orange-peel look we get on the thighs and bottom that makes us embarrassed to strip off by the pool, let alone in that long-awaited romantic clinch.

cellulite

Many doubting Thomas scientists still believe cellulite to be another word for 'fat', dreamt up French cosmetic companies to help them sell more products. Yet any woman who currently battles against dimply skin will be pleased to know that it is not as simple as that.

The good news is that there is a growing band of enlightened doctors who are taking its presence and treatment seriously. In order to do so, they have had to find out what makes cellulite different to ordinary fat and what causes it to develop.

According to cellulite expert Dr Elizabeth Dancy, cellulite is caused through normal fat cells and the fine fibres surrounding them becoming damaged due to a lack of nutrients and a build up of toxins.

Both problems stem from a poor blood supply to the layers of fat just under the skin. Blood flowing into the fat cells should bring with it a range of vitamins, minerals and oxygen to feed the fat cells, the fine fibres surrounding them and a system called the lymphatic system that takes take away waste toxins like carbon dioxide.

The blood vessels in question are not the large main arteries you find flowing from the heart and into various organs, but their small branches called capillaries. It is the tiny capillaries that carry blood directly up to individual cells throughout the whole body, including fat cells.

If the circulation of blood to and through the capillaries is not good and the walls of the capillaries are not strong, naturally the supply of nutrients and oxygen to the fat cells and fine fibres dries up. At the same time, the transportation away of toxins slows up so that in turn they build up.

The lack of nourishment and toxin build up soon causes the fine fibres surrounding fat cells to develop into tough fibrous knots. This means that instead of the fat cells sliding over each other and moving quite freely under the skin, they become trapped within and between the knots. This is what produces the dimpled look of the fat under the skin – the dimples we know as cellulite.

The key to conquering cellulite and preventing more from developing therefore involves improving the blood supply to and away from the layers of fat just under the skin. Taking regular exercise is vital for this. Not only Jon's plan, but making sure that you move around at every opportunity to increase general activity and get those muscles, and therefore the circulation, going.

conquering **cellulite**

diet

The walls of the capillaries are extremely thin. If they become damaged and leaky, they can neither deliver to nor take away substances from fat cells.

Parts of their walls are made from collagen, a sort of cement, which gives them structure. A lack of antioxidant nutrients such as vitamin C can lead to a weakening of collagen. Other plant nutrients called bioflavonoids, particularly anthocyanidins, help to strengthen collagen. Making sure that you regularly eat plenty of these nutrients is therefore an important part of any anti-cellulite campaign.

Vitamin C is found in citrus fruits such as oranges and grapefruit, kiwi fruit, berries either fresh or frozen, paw paw and vegetables, in particular peppers and dark green leafy vegetables like spinach and cabbage. As for bioflavanoids, they are distributed among the fruit and vegetable world, so make sure as many Love Bites as possible are made up from the fruit section and pile on extra vegetables whenever you can. Anthocyanidins are more specifically found in dark blue berries, the richest source being bilberries.

Eating a diet that reduces the chances of cholesterol blocking your blood vessels is also important. Blockages narrow the vessels and reduce the flow of blood. Drastically cutting back on saturated fats, found in animal foods like fatty meats, meat products such as burgers and pies, as well as biscuits, cakes and cream, can help to reduce cholesterol levels in the blood.

the three Cs

It is also necessary to pay attention to the three Cs – constipation, clothes and caffeine – when trying to give our veins and lymph fluid the best chance of carrying toxins and carbon dioxide away from fat cells under the skin.

Straining to go the loo when you are constipated slows down the flow of lymph fluid, while tight trousers, hold-ups and tight underwear, especially when sitting down, can squash the veins and lymphatic system, which are trying valiantly to pump away their contents.

Too many coffees, teas, cola drinks and cold remedies can also be a problem because the caffeine they contain has the effect of constricting blood vessels – the last thing you want when you are trying to improve blood flow. Most cellulite experts recommend sticking to no more than a couple of caffeine-containing drinks a day.

eight-point, cellulite-beating diet plan

The best approach to beating cellulite is to tackle it from various angles, of which diet is just one.

Obviously though, it is an important one and the best advice is based on following a set of concepts for the rest of your life. To some extent they reflect what we have covered earlier in the book but they do require you to be stricter with yourself and to select Love Bites that are not sugary or fatty.

1 **Reduce the amount of fat that you eat,** especially the ones that are saturated and are by definition solid at room temperature. In practice this means keeping the fat on meat and in cheese, butter and lard to a minimum. The same approach applies to foods that contain these things, for instance cakes, biscuits, pastry, burgers, sausages and many fast food and ready meal options.

2 Although you are cutting back on the total amount of fat you eat and foods rich in saturated animal fats, **you need some of the essential fats found in oily fish, nuts and seeds.** These help to reduce the chances of blood clotting and sticking to blood vessel walls, which makes them narrower and inhibits the free flow of blood.

3 **Salt.** Ok, so salt does not contain calories, but when we eat too much it can increase the amount of water our bodies retain. This can lead to obvious bloating but it also may result in the less obvious retention of water between fat cells, which slows blood flow and makes cellulite look worse. Cutting back on processed foods is the most effective way of reducing salt intake, although

not adding it during cooking and at the table is also helpful. It will take a few weeks to get used to the dramatic reduction in your salt intake, but your taste buds do adapt.

4 **Go really easy on extra sugar.** Dr Karen Burke, an American cellulite expert, tells us that sugar leads to the release of the hormone insulin, which grabs sugar out of the blood and then delivers it into the fat cells to be stored as fat. Karen advises people to avoid obvious sugar slugs, such as those in tea and coffee, and also to give a wide berth to hidden sources, which include foods like milkshakes, biscuits, cakes and, of course, sweets.

5 **Select hard foods.** These are fruits and vegetables that supply plenty of antioxidant vitamins, minerals and plant nutrients, which keep capillaries and veins healthy, along with fibre, which cuts your chances of becoming constipated.

6 **Go for protein foods in every meal.** Not only do they help to fill you up, but they do not trigger the release of the fat storing hormone insulin.

7 **Avoid alcohol and caffeine.** Alcohol supplies extra calories and caffeine, as we know, constricts blood vessels.

8 Last and not least is to **drink loads and loads of water.** It helps to curb hunger between meals and, with the fibre you eat, bulks out the stools and makes them easy to pass.

exercise

For a strong supply of blood full of nutrients and oxygen to the capillaries, exercise is crucial. Getting your heart rate up and thus your blood pumping more forcefully through your arteries and capillaries helps to keep them elastic and in good shape.

Exercise not only improves the delivery of nutrients and oxygen, but also helps the veins and lymphatic system to pump waste products away from the fatty parts of our bodies. Veins quite literally have to push blood and the carbon dioxide and toxins it contains uphill, taking them to the lungs and liver to be made safe and be removed from the body.

Muscles help with this battle against gravity. Every time they contract, they help to force the contents of veins and lymph fluid back up towards the heart. The calf muscles are the most important muscles in this process, so exercising them regularly through walking, trotting up and down the stairs and jogging certainly helps.

There is also an area of the foot, which has an important role in helping lymph fluid to keep moving away up and from your fat cells. The area runs between your heel and the base of your toes. Keeping it stimulated, again through walking and particularly dancing, is very important in any anti-cellulite plan. So too is good breathing technique and posture.

breathing

It might be hard to see how breathing is linked to cellulite. But here are the facts. When you breathe, the muscle under your lungs called the diaphragm should contract. This causes a sucking action in the surrounding veins and lymphatic system, helping to pull them back towards the lungs and heart.

Lots of people do not take good deep breaths right down into their bellies that use the diaphragm, but instead take shallow, short breaths that only use the upper part of the chest.

To start belly breathing and getting your diaphragm working well, breathe in gently through your nose. Pause and then breathe out. Do it slowly and when you breathe in, push your belly out. Make sure that as you are breathing in and out, your tummy is also moving in and out.

In order for belly breathing and good diaphragm movement to become the norm, you need to practise. Dr John Briffa, who is the author of a book called *BodyWise* (Cima), recommends taking ten good belly breaths three times a day to get the process started. It should then soon become second nature.

The sooner it does so the better because belly breathing also increases the amount of oxygen we take in, making more available to all cells in the body, including fat cells. The more oxygen that gets to them, the more able the fat cells are to burn up their stores and for you to lose weight.

smoking

Smoking is another no-no. We all know that it causes lung cancer, but the nicotine it pumps into the system also constricts blood vessels throughout the body.

posture

If we stand with our pelvis and tummy tilted forwards and our bottoms sticking out, the flow of blood and lymph up from the legs through the pelvis is badly affected. Learning to stand correctly with the tummy and bottom tucked in and the pelvis in the right position is therefore important.

cellulite-busting exercise plan

It is important to follow Jon's daily exercise routine to help burn fat and improve posture. Finding time to do much more is going to be tough but, if you can, try to fit in some extra stretches at the end of every session.

Stretching is crucial because, as Dr Karen Burke tells us, it is a way of elongating your muscles to give them the appearance of being longer and leaner and to help to flatten out the dimply layer of fat, thereby diminishing the appearance of cellulite.

front thigh

To really stretch out the main big muscle that runs down the front of the upper part of your leg (known as the quadriceps), first find a chair. Hold onto the back of it with your left hand to balance yourself and bend your right knee so that your right leg comes up behind you. Grab the ankle of the right foot and, pointing your knee down, hold it like that for 30 seconds. Repeat on the other leg and then do both legs one more time.

back thigh

To elongate the back thigh muscle (called the hamstring), from standing, bend your left knee and take your right foot out in front of you. Rest your hands on your right thigh. Lift the toe of the right foot off the ground until you can feel the stretch along the back of the leg. Hold for 30 seconds then repeat on the other leg. Do both legs one more time.

lower leg stretch

To stretch out the muscle in the back of your lower leg (the calf), you need to stand with your right leg in front of your left. Keeping both feet on the ground, slowly bend the right leg so that the knee is at right angles and you can feel a stretch in the left calf. Hold for 30 seconds and repeat on the other leg. Do both legs once more.

treatments
aromatherapy

Essential oils extracted from plants are readily absorbed via the skin and into the blood. Applied locally to the affected area, aromatherapy should be used in conjunction with other treatments. Special formulations for tackling cellulite can be obtained through an aromatherapist. Rubbed gently and smoothly into the skin in a fan-like upwards movement, the essential oils selected will help to improve the workings of the veins, the lymph system, the microcirculation and the fat-releasing process itself.

A particularly useful combination of essential oils appears to be a mix of 2 ml each of evergreen cypress, citrus limon, Atlantic cedar, sage and eucalyptus, in 90 ml of hazelnut carrier oil. This can be rubbed in three times a day. It is not suitable for those with breast disease or pregnant women.

anti-cellulite creams and gels

Useful for helping to treat the earlier signs of cellulite, these creams and gels can, in Dr Dancy's opinion, be beneficial when used in conjunction with diet and exercise: 'They help to improve the quality of the skin and prevent the development of further cellulite.'

The main active ingredients to look for in these products are listed here, along with the functions they are said to perform.

Hedera helix	This extract of ivy has a decongesting effect on tissues.
Centella asiatica	An extract of the wild chestnut plant, it helps to strengthen the walls of the veins, thereby helping to stop fluid leaking into the fatty cells. It also

stimulates fibroblasts – the cells that repair damaged tissues in the cellulite.

Caffeine

Not recommended for internal consumption when trying to rid the body of cellulite, yet paradoxically, when applied directly to the skin it is said to stimulate receptors on the surface of the fat cells, helping them to release their contents into the bloodstream.

Aminophylline

Like caffeine, this substance helps stimulate the release of fat into the bloodstream.

Silicum

This helps to protect small blood vessels and improves blood supply, even when tissues have developed cellulite.

Hazelnut oil

This oil has decongestive properties and vitamin E, which helps protect fatty cells from attack by damaging free radicals.

Thiomucase

This is an enzyme taken – wait for it – from the testicles of bulls. Despite its rather unsavoury source, for those with cellulite it can be mightily useful. It is thought to help break up the thickened fibres in cellulite tissue and is useful on large areas of cellulite.

anti-cellulite supplements

Elizabeth Dancy recommends certain supplements to

help in the battle against cellulite. While none has undergone clinical trials to prove that it is definitely effective, each has known actions in the body that provide a rationale for thinking that they may have a beneficial role to play in beating the lumpy-bumpies.

Centella asiatica   This can be taken in supplement form as well as being found in creams and gels. Six 100-mg tablets are recommended daily. Again, it helps to strengthen the veins.

Seaweed extracts   Containing iodine, when taken as a supplement kelp and fucus are said to help stimulate the metabolism. Never exceed the recommended dose as advised on the packaging. Too much can be harmful.

Ginkgo biloba   Known to strengthen small veins and arteries, it may help strengthen weak veins and aid poor circulation in the legs. Follow pack instructions. One of the best products is called 'Ginkyo' and is known to supply a standardized extract of the Ginkgo plant's active components.

Vitis vinifera   Grape extracts that contain flavonoids and tannins, thought to improve blood flow in the microcirculation.

Artichoke   Standardized extracts of artichoke are

said to help to promote the removal of fat from fat cells and have detoxifying properties. Cynara Artichoke one-a-day capsules by Lichtwer Pharma with standardized extracts of Cynara scolymus is one popular product available in many health food shops.

Horsetail Contains silicium which is thought to strengthen the walls of the small arteries and veins.

skin brushing

This home treatment improves the look of the skin rather than getting to the root of the cellulite problem itself. Since we are after some quick fixes over the next 15 days, I think it's a must. What nicer way to boost your confidence than feeling your skin is at its smoothest, softest and looking as vibrantly glowing as possible?

By helping to kick-start the circulation and the drainage of lymph fluid, it is important that skin brushing is done gently with a special brush that does not pull the skin. Taking just 5 – 10 minutes a day, fit in a session of skin brushing after a bath, starting at the ankles and using gentle motions upwards. Being rough just damages the microcirculation and is not helpful. After skin brushing, anti-cellulite creams or aromatherapy oils can be gently massaged in.

ionothermie

This needs to be carried out by a professional. The treatment involves applying clay to the affected areas, then applying electrical currents which allow the active compounds in clay to pass into the skin and help to tone the muscles. It is good for catching early stages of cellulite and freshens the look of the skin. Sessions cost approximately £175 for the first course of five weekly treatments. They are then about £35 for a monthly session of 1 hour and 15 minutes. While you might not have the time or cash for a full course of treatment, you can at least get started and finish them off after your holidays or first date.

manual lymphatic drainage

This is a very gentle form of massage that should only be performed by someone who has undergone specialist training. The actions of the masseur drain and pump the cellulite, helping to relieve congestion and improve circulation to the areas with cellulite. Sessions cost approximately £45 for each one-hour session. One hour twice a week for three weeks is recommended, followed by one session a month for maintenance. If you have only got 15 days then you have got time to fit in four.

mesotherapy

This involves a medically trained doctor injecting specific medicines into the affected areas. About four sessions are needed to see changes, with a total of 10 to 15 required in total. Silica, extracts of artichoke, chickweed and minerals such as manganese and copper and the enzyme thiomucase may also be used. Again, it is more of a long-term approach to treatment, but you could get some sessions underway over the next two weeks.

other crucial quick fixes for looking, feeling and smelling sexy

teeth

Yellow, stained teeth are a turn-off. Smoking and drinking strong tea, coffee and red wine all contribute to the problem. You can go to see the dental hygienist at your dentist's surgery for advice on the best way to approach the problem. He or she may suggest a good cleaning session at the surgery, and will be able to advise you about whitening toothpastes that can help to keep the teeth white and sparkling. Professional tooth-whitening companies also exist and may be worth checking out if your problem is severe. Learn how to floss to keep your gums healthy, and start chewing sugar-free gum after meals. Choose brands that contain Xylitol. This sugar-free sweetener helps to fight decay and keep the mouth fresh, clean and invitingly and irresistibly kissable.

personal hygiene

OK, so it's a pretty obvious one – but do keep yourself sparklingly clean and smelling fresh. If you know you perspire heavily, then invest in a good antiperspirant/ deodorant. Individual choices of perfumes and after-shaves are up to you, but one word of caution: don't go overboard. Give some of your natural pheromones a chance to come through.

nails

Clean well-manicured nails are a must. They may be a small detail but they are one that shows you have taken time and pride in your appearance. It shows you think you are worth it, and if you believe this, so will others around you. Treat yourself to a personal mani-cure before your holiday or big date. If you really want to go for the complete look , push the boat out with a pedicure, too. There is nothing worse than gnarled-up feet with hard skin and poorly kept nails.

If professional treatments are not an option, make time to do a homespun job. If you do not feel confident about doing this yourself, you might be lucky enough to have a good friend who will oblige. Manicure and pedicure sets are available from chemists.

Remember, this one is *not* just for the girls. Boys' grooming kits contain gadgets and gizmos for keeping hands and feet looking good. Nicely kept nails are, like so many things in life now, no longer strictly within a female's domain.

bad breath

Another unfortunate complaint that will have even the most dedicated admirer wondering whether they want to get into a full clinch with you. An infection of the gums is one of the main causes of this problem. Your dentist must treat this. He or she must also treat any gingivitis, an inflammation of the gums.

Stomach problems such as a hiatus hernia can also cause smelly breath, as can infections of the tonsils. A lack of saliva – caused, for example, by dehydration – may be responsible, as could a food allergy where certain components of the diet remain undigested in the gut, creating odours that are refluxed up into the mouth and then appear on the breath. Check out any possible digestive disorders with your doctor.

Brushing your teeth twice a day, daily flossing and regular trips to the dentist can help reduce the risk of bad breath. Antibacterial mouth washes used before you brush your teeth can help reduce plaque and possible odours.

Crash dieting – when energy intakes are less than 1,000 calories a day – can also cause halitosis. This just goes to show that a steadier approach is well worth embracing. Also bear in mind that constipation can lead to bad breath. A diet rich in fruits, vegetables and wholegrain cereals, combined with good fluid intakes, can reduce the risk of constipation.

a helping hand:

weird and wonderful **weight-loss products**

Walk into a health food store or check out the ads in newspapers and magazines and a host of weight-loss products will be ready and waiting to grab both your attention and hard-earned cash. There are plenty to choose from, including those that claim to fill you up, ones that say they turn off hunger and even some that would have you believe you slim while you sleep. 'Dream on,' you might feel like saying.

In addition to all the amazing weight-loss pills and potions on offer you will also see information on various machines that miraculously make your flabby bits vanish into thin air. Before and after photos are usually enough to get you reaching for your wallet.

On top of all of these gadgets and gizmos come the hard medical-style prescription drugs designed to help shed pounds. Some are considered perfectly safe; others tend only to be available from so-called 'slimming clinics' that should know better.

It's easy to bundle all of these products together and dismiss them as a waste of time and money; but is this perhaps being slightly unfair? Could some of them actually work? Should we believe what the manufacturers tell us? Some certainly contain ingredients that sound as though they should work, and often there has been work carried out in laboratories to show that, in theory at least, they have certain effects on the absorption and use of the nutrients we eat. Many have never been proven to work in humans.

The fact that you have spent money and then begin to use these products might be just what you need to provide that much-needed bit of support to boost morale and keep you on the right track. It may keep you eating well and doing your exercise program even if in reality they do little to speed your metabolism or block fat digestion. You could say, then, that so long as they are not dangerous they have a role to play in offering a helping hand, even if it is via a placebo effect, in the battle with the bulge.

In this chapter you can take a closer look at what's on offer and what the manufacturers tell us their products can do. This is accompanied by the expert opinion of Dr Susan Jebb. A well-known obesity expert, Susan is Head of Nutrition at the Medical Research Council's Human Nutrition Research in Cambridge, England, and aims to fills us in with the scientific background, to help us know whether there is any good research to prove what the manufacturers want us to believe.

substances that affect **energy metabolism**

Your metabolic rate determines the speed at which calories are burned. The most simple and effective way of improving on your metabolic rate is through increasing exercise and making your muscles work more effectively.

Certain drugs such as nicotine also increase your rate of metabolism, although since smoking has such bad negative health effects, clearly it is not to be advised. Recently there has been a rush to develop products containing minerals, amino acids and plant extracts to do the job more naturally. Here are some you will find on the supplement shelves.

chromium
what is it?

Chromium is a mineral which the body needs to help control blood sugar levels. It works closely with the hormone insulin, helping to determine just how much glucose is taken into cells and how much is taken off to be converted into, and stored as, fat. Low chromium levels are said to reduce the action of insulin and possibly lead to an increase in blood sugar levels.

what is it supposed to do?

Dubbed by optimum nutritionist Patrick Holford as the 'metabolism mineral', studies suggest that taking chromium may enhance the body's ability to burn fat. Chromium picolinate is the form of this mineral that is often recommended for such purposes, in doses of around 200 micrograms (mcg) of per day. This is more than you will find in most normal diets, however 'healthy' they are.

susan says

Some but not all studies have suggested that long-term chromium supplementation may have modest benefits on the glucose/insulin system in patients with diabetes. However, in people who do not have diabetes there is little evidence of any real benefit from chromium supplementation.

Some studies on animals have suggested that long-term supplementation with chromium may increase the proportion of lean tissue and decrease the proportion of fat. However, this is usually only seen in growing animals. There is much less evidence that chromium supplementation in humans is able to affect body composition. The most effective method for adult men and women to increase muscle mass is resistance training. Most studies have shown no additional benefit of chromium supplementation. Most studies of chromium supplements taken during a weight-loss program have not shown any effect on weight loss or body composition.

Like many micronutrients that are essential in small quantities, large quantities of chromium can be toxic. There are reports of anaemia and liver and kidney dysfunction following high-dose chromium supplementation (1,200 mcg a day) over several months.

should anyone avoid it?

Pregnant and breastfeeding women and anyone on medication should check with their doctor before taking any chromium supplement.

Products Available

Product	Manufacturer	Provides
B13 Chromium	Larkhall Green Farm	200 mcg chromium orotate per tablet
Chromium picolinate Vegicaps	Solgar	500 mcg trivalent chromium in a vegetable-based capsule

hca

what is it?

HCA is the shortened version of the supplement called hydroxycitrate. This is extracted from the rind of the tamarind fruit (*Garcinia cambogia*). About the size of an orange, tamarinds have a thin skin that contains around 30% HCA. Grown in southern India, the fruit is dried and used in curries.

what is it supposed to do?

HCA is said to be capable of blocking the production of fat from carbohydrate foods, a feat that has been proven in animals but not yet in humans. It also appears to help reduce appetite in animals. It does not seem to block the fat-storing mechanisms involved in converting fats in the diet into body fat, so if it works at all, it should be used alongside a low-fat diet. Holford recommends a supplement of 250 mg of HCA three times a day, while naturopathic doctor and author Michael T Murray suggests 500 mg three times a day and believes that its effect will be enhanced when taken with chromium.

susan says

HCA has generated considerable interest because of the strong evidence from animal studies that it can block some of the pathways through which carbohydrate is converted to fat. However, an excellent study recently published which looked closely at the effects of HCA in 135 overweight men and women attending an obesity clinic at a top New York hospital showed no effect whatsoever on the weight of those taking HCA supplements compared to those taking a placebo (dummy) treatment.

should anyone avoid it?

Pregnant and breastfeeding women and anyone on medication should check with their doctor before taking HCA.

products available

Product	Manufacturer	Provides
Citrimax	Holland and Barrett	Two tablets supply 750 mg of HCA from *Garcinia cambogia* Two tablets to be taken daily, one before breakfast and one before lunch
Hydroxy Citrate Vegicaps	Solgar	Each 310-mg capsule supplies 250 mg of HCA

L-carnitine
what is it?

L-carnitine is an amino acid which is made in the body from two other amino acids called methionine and lysine. It is involved in the utilization and metabolism of fats. It helps stimulate the secretion of fat burning enzymes and also helps maintain muscle tone.

what is it supposed to do?

It has been proposed that an inadequate amount of L-carnitine in the body may diminish fat-burning capabilities and that supplementing the diet with this amino acid at levels of 250 mg three times a day after meals could help weight loss.

susan says

Carnitine plays a central role in fatty acid metabolism, transporting fatty acids into the mitochondrial cells where they can be oxidized (burned). It has been widely suggested that carnitine may improve physical performance, but the evidence is equivocal. There is even less evidence that it has any role in helping to burn fat or increase rates of weight loss.

should anyone avoid it?

Pregnant and breast-feeding women and people with kidney problems.

products available

Product	Manufacturer	Provides
Slim-nite	Reevecrest Healthcare	25 mg of L-carnitine per capsule. Three to be taken before going to bed
Maxi L-Carnitine	Solgar	Each 500-mg tablet supplies 500 mg L-carnitine
L-Carnitine	Larkhall Green Farm	Each 250-mg supplies 250 mg L-carnitine

l-arginine

what is it?

L-arginine is an amino acid that can be manufactured in the body and is involved in, among other things, the metabolism of carbohydrate.

what is it supposed to do?

Manufacturers of diet supplement products containing L-arginine tell us that these products play an important role in the body's metabolism. L-arginine is said to stimulate muscle growth and the burning of fat.

susan says

There is no evidence in healthy subjects of a deficiency in arginine, since the body is able to make it from other protein foods.

should anyone avoid it?

People with the herpes simplex virus infection should avoid L-arginine supplements, as should pregnant and breastfeeding women.

products available

Product	Manufacturer	Provides
Slim-nite	Reevecrest Healthcare	250 mg L-arginine per capsule. Three to be taken prior to going to sleep

| L-Arginine Quest | 500 mg L-arginine per 500-mg capsule. One to four capsules daily on an empty stomach |
| L-Arginine Solgar Vegicaps | 500 mg L-arginine per 500-mg capsule |

creatine
what is it?

Creatine is needed for the production of energy within the cells and is concentrated in the skeletal muscles. Exercise depletes creatine.

what is it supposed to do?

Supplements of creatine are said to restore levels and help re-energize the muscles, allowing you to exercise more. By helping you sustain maximum power for longer you can train for longer, and creatine is said to help you lose more fat when you exercise regularly.

susan says

There is some evidence to suggest that creatine-loading using creatine supplements may enhance muscular performance and prolong endurance. However, there is no evidence that creatine supplementation is associated with increased losses of weight or fat. Few people trying to control their weight actually exercise to exhaustion – most run out of time or enthusiasm first.

Product	Manufacturer	Provides
Multipower	Creatine Instant	500-g sachets

5-HTP

what is it?

5-HTP is the name for the compound 5-hydroxytryptophan from which the brain's 'happy neurotransmitter' called serotonin is made.

what is it supposed to do?

Serotonin is said to reduce the appetite. Manufacturers of 5-HTP say it is able to help natural weight loss.

susan says

Serotonin is one of the neurotransmitters in the brain that is involved in feelings of hunger and fullness. High levels of serotonin in the hypothalamus of the brain are known to suppress appetite. However, 5-HTP is produced naturally in the body from the amino acid tryptophan, which is found in most protein-containing foods. Most people consume more than sufficient quantities of protein, even whilst dieting. There is no evidence that taking additional supplements of 5-HTP will have any affect on body weight.

products available

Product	Manufacturer	Provides
Health & Diet 5-HTP	Tri-medica	50-mg tablets

metabolic **stimulants**

susan says

For all the metabolic stimulants: Some chemical compounds, including ephedrine, caffeine and nicotine, can act as metabolic stimulants, boosting the metabolic rate. However, in order to increase metabolic rate it is necessary for the cells of the body to take up more oxygen. This means that more blood has to be transported to the cells, and to do so the heart rate must be increased. At higher doses there may also be an increase in blood pressure. As the dose is increased these side-effects become unpleasant and ultimately dangerous. Some people seem to be particularly sensitive to these effects. Nonetheless, ephedrine/caffeine mixtures have been shown to produce slightly greater weight loss than placebo in controlled clinical trails. Some studies have suggested that these compounds may also have some appetite-suppressing effects since the weight loss observed is slightly greater than predicted from the effects on energy expenditure alone.

ephedra (ma huang)

what is it?

Ephedra is a herb also known as Ma huang that contains the active ingredient ephedrine, which is structurally similar to amphetamines.

what is it supposed to do?

It is said to help speed up the metabolism and cause weight loss, particularly when taken with caffeine. Such preparations are available in the US, but Ephedra is banned in the UK.

who should avoid it?

Ephedra has been linked to many incidents of causing high blood pressure, severe headaches, heart beat abnormalities, seizures, heart attacks and even death, which is why it is banned in the UK. Clearly everyone should avoid it.

caffeine

what is it?

Technically speaking, caffeine belongs to a group of substances known as 'methyl xanthins' which are capable of stimulating the heart and central nervous system.

what is it supposed to do?

Consumption of caffeine has been shown to lead to a temporary increase in the metabolic rate and the rate at which fat is broken down. Some studies show that this happens in a dose-dependent manner, which means the more coffee you drink, the greater this effect.

Even so, the total number of calories caffeine burns is so small that it is probably insignificant. For general health, no more than six cups of caffeine-containing drinks such as coffee, tea and colas are recommended daily. Aside from its effects on the metabolic rate of the body, caffeine may help the body to burn fat when taken in conjunction with exercise. So if you are going to drink coffee, this means that you may as well make the most of its potential fat-burning effects and get up off your bottoms and start getting active.

Recent research suggests that giving 200 – 600 mg of caffeine (that is about two – six cups of filtered coffee), about 30 minutes before aerobic exercise, increases the amount of fat that is broken down from our body stores to fuel the working muscles. This only works when you are not drinking much other caffeine during the day, and save your 'shot' for the time just prior to exercise.

Probably the best advice is to not overdo caffeine-rich drinks such as coffee, colas and tea and to save them for times when you really feel you need a lift. Perhaps, for example, have one or two cups of tea or coffee to get you going in the morning, the same mid-afternoon, and again prior to exercise.

who should avoid it?

Too much caffeine can cause increases in blood pressure and heart rate as well as insomnia, irritability and anxiety. Some people are more sensitive to it than others. Those who are stressed and anxious should avoid large intakes.

guarana
what is it?

Guarana grows wild in the Amazon jungle. Local South Americans use it for its energy-giving powers and its ability to revitalize the body.

what is it supposed to do?

Sold as a fat burner and metabolism booster, guarana is available in capsules, drinks and even sweets. It contains a variety of methyl xanthins including caffeine. These stimulants are said to be released gradually into the blood, unlike the caffeine in coffee that is absorbed quickly and is said to improve metabolism over time.

who should avoid it?

Guarana is a stimulant and is best avoided by those who suffer with anxiety, stress or heart conditions.

products available

Product	Manufacturer	Provides
Shrinkers Chrome Plus 'The Natural Aid for Slimmers'	Swiss Health	67 mcg of ChromePlus, a blend of chromium polynicolinate and oxygen-balanced niacin plus bladderwrack, guarana, peppermint, Siberian ginseng, ginger root, capsicum, chamomile, liquorice root
Trim-Maxx Burners 'The Ultimate Aid to Burning Fat'	Body Breakthrough	Contains 500 mg HCA, 200 mcg chromium polynicolinate plus choline, inositol, methionine, L-carnitine, vitamin B_6, iodine, bromelain, buchu leaves, uva ursi, cranberry concentrate, ginseng, Essential Fatty Acids and pantethine
14-Day Fat Metaboliser 'Lose Weight Fast'	Schiff	125 mg HCA, 5 mg L-carnitine and L-tartrate, 2.5 mg caffeine, 2.5 mg arbutin, 2.5 mg cayenne powder, 1.25 mg vitamin B_6 and 100 mcg of chromium

| Diet System 6 | Passion International Ltd | 1,500 mg Citrimax containing HCA, 300 mcg of chromium picolinate, choline bitartrate, inositol, betaine GCL, kola nut extract, ginger, guarana and L-carnitine |
| More than a Diet | Holland and Barrett | 100 mcg of chromium, 550 mg Citrimax containing HCA, L-carnitine, capsicum ginger, liquorice, mustard seed, ginseng, kola nut, guarana, oat bran fibre, Essential Fatty Acids, spirulina and much, much more |

There are other substances found within the plant world that are said to increase the metabolic rate. These include capsicum in chillies and hot peppers, extracts from the Kola nut, mustard seed extracts, and ginger extracts.

There is no evidence however that any of these actually help encourage fat to be burned and weight to be lost.

products that help fill you up and **reduce hunger**

Some products are sold on the basis that they help you slim through making you feel full. Most of these are based on fibre-like substances.

susan says

For all the fibre products: Fibre comes in many forms. Some types of fibre reduce the rate at which food passes through the digestive tract, some decrease blood cholesterol levels, others increase the bulk of the faeces. Some particular types of fibre, known as prebiotics, promote the growth of beneficial bacterial in the gut, which help to maintain a healthy digestive system. Most people in Britain consume far less than the recommended 18 g of fibre per day, and so incorporating more into our diets we are likely to help improve health in many different ways.

When it comes to weight loss, high-fibre diets, incorporating plenty of fibre-rich foods such as fruits, vegetables and complex carbohydrates may be a useful dieting aid as they provide added bulk to meals. You can fill your plate with low-calorie fibre-rich foods and not feel deprived. This makes it easier to eat fewer calories without feeling hungry. However there is very little evidence that taking fibre supplements gives the same results. Some studies show a short-term reduction in food consumed, but in the longer term most people find their bodies adapt to the added bulk in the digestive system and the fibre supplements have no lasting effect on the rate of weight loss.

glucomannan

what is it?

Glucomannan is a type of fibre taken from the root of an East Asian plant called the 'konjac plant'.

what is it supposed to do?

It is said to absorb 10 times as much water as wheat bran and that when taken in capsule form with a glass of water one hour prior to eating can help to reduce your appetite.

Glucomannan can be bought in 500-mg capsules. Manufacturers suggest taking one to two capsules an hour before meals.

who should avoid it?

Check with your doctor that it is safe for you to take glucomannan before doing so.

products available

Product	Provides
Cantassium Glucomannan 500	Each tablet contains 500 mg of glucomannan. 1 – 2 tablets to be taken an hour before main meals with at least a cup of water

guar gum
what is it?

Guar gum is a type of water-absorbing fibre extracted from the cluster bean. It is commonly added to
yoghurts as a thickener and is used in the pharmaceutical industry to help slow down the absorption
of drugs. Research has shown that when included in
foods such as bread, guar gum helps to slow down
the rise in blood sugar. It may therefore be helpful
for people with diabetes in controlling their blood
sugar levels.

what is it supposed to do?

For slimmers, guar gum is supposed to be useful
because it is said to absorb water in the stomach,
expand and create a feeling of fullness.

who should avoid it?

There is a risk of guar gum swelling up in the throat or
intestines and causing blockages. Anyone with swallowing difficulties or gastrointestinal problems should
avoid guar gum. It can also lead to excruciating wind.

Guar gum is not easily available, although your
pharmacist may be able to get supplies of it.

psyllium husks
what are they?

The husks from the seeds of the plantain plant.
Herbalists have known for centuries that the seeds act

as laxatives, and they are used today by pharmaceutical companies to make laxatives that bulk out the stools.

what are they supposed to do?

Capsules or powder made from the husks of the seeds are available; it is recommended that they be taken before and after eating to help create a feeling of fullness. The capsules or powder do this by binding with water in the stomach. The idea is that they help you to reduce the amount of food and thus calories consumed.

who should avoid them?

Anyone with throat or oesophagus problems and swallowing difficulties.

products available

Product	Manufacturer	Provides
Psyllium husk capsules	Larkhall Green Farm	Provide 350 mg of powdered psyllium per capsule. 2 – 3 are advised before and after main meals with a full glass of water
Psyllium husks	Holland and Barrett	500-mg capsules supplying 500 mg psyllium. 2 capsules to be taken with water
Psyllium seed husks	Solgar	Each level tablespoon provides 5.8 g psyllium husk fibre

other fibres

Products said to help aid weight-loss as part of a calorie-controlled diet include mixes of corn bran, barley bran, citrus fibre concentrate, inulin sugar beet fibre concentrate, soya fibre, apple pectin and methylcellulose.

products available

Product	Manufacturer	Provides
Fibre Diet	Holland and Barrett	440 mg of fibre per tablet coming from sugar beet, soya beans and citrus fruit
Vita Fibre	Peter Black Healthcare Ltd	422 mg of fibre per tablet coming from corn bran, barley bran, orange fibre concentrate, inulin, sugar beet concentrate and methylcellulose
Bran Slim	Thompson Medical Company Ltd	Sachets of hot chocolate-flavoured instant drink mix. Each sachet supplies 6 grams of fibre coming from soya fibre and inulin

fat **blockers**

chitosan

what is it?

Chitosan is made from chitin, a type of fibre that is similar in structure to cellulose and is found in mushrooms as well as the shells of crabs, shrimp and other shellfish. When 'cooked', chitin changes its structure and is turned into a substance known as chitosan.

what is it supposed to do?

The cooking process is said to give chitosan molecules a positive charge which gives them magnet-like properties, attracting fatty acids. These fatty acids are the building blocks of fat and bile acids used to make cholesterol. When fatty acids or bile acids come near chitosan, the chitosan grabs them and holds tightly on. Instead of the fatty acids being used to build fat stores or the bile acids being converted into cholesterol, the chitosan is said to form an indigestible blob that passes through the intestines and out of the body in the stools. In effect, chitosan seems to block fat digestion.

When chitosan is added to hot water and butter is added, the chitosan and butter can be seen to form lumps. The same is true when chitosan is added to milk or to a creamy liqueur such as Baileys. This, claim some scientists, proves chitosan's fat-binding properties.

Researchers tell us that for each 450-gram capsule containing 350 mg of chitosan consumed half an hour before a meal, at least 3 grams of fat will pass through your body undigested. As an example, this means that taking 4 capsules of chitosan before a meal should bind 12 grams of fat, so that 108 calories pass through your body as though you had not eaten them.

susan says

A controlled clinical trial of chitosan supplementation in humans has recently been published. It showed no weight loss whatsoever in a group of overweight women who were prescribed 8 chitosan tablets per day for 4 weeks. This is in contrast to a number of other studies that have been carried out in a test-tube or in animal studies, which suggested that chitosan may accelerate the rate of weight loss. These discrepancies may be explained by the fact that proving fatty acids bind to chitosan in a test-tube does not prove that this happens in the body. Also, the dose of chitosan given in animal studies is approximately 15 – 22 times greater than recommended for humans. Previous human studies have also included a low-calorie diet program alongside the chitosan treatment; it is likely that the diet contributed to the weight loss observed in earlier human studies.

who should avoid it?

People allergic to shellfish.

products available

Product	Manufacturer	Provides
Fat Magnets	Fat Magnets International Ltd	Each 450-mg capsule supplies 350g of ChitosanPlex. 2 – 4 are recommended, to be taken prior to meals along with plenty of water
X-Fat	X-Fat UK Ltd	A chitosan suspension that comes in 14.8 ml sachets, supplying 4 g of chitosan per serving. Should be added to a small amount of water or fruit juice and taken after meals, as opposed to pills and powder forms that are taken prior to meals. A glass of water should be taken after.
Fat Bonda with Chitosan	Larkhall Green Farm	Contains 85% chitosan per 300-mg tablet. 2 – 4 tablets to be taken when eating meals containing fat

other weight-loss **products**

scented pens

what are they?

AromaScent Diet Pens have been impregnated with aromas that you sniff when feeling hungry.

what are they supposed to do?

Research reveals that our hunger centres in the brain are stimulated by smell. The idea is that you sniff your pen prior to eating and this helps to trigger the 'I'm full' parts of your brain and thereby helps you control your appetite and food intake.

susan says

The thought, smell and general anticipation of food all contribute to our appetite. Smells of food we enjoy can boost appetite and stimulate feelings of hunger. It is plausible that repeated exposure to the same smell can ultimately dull the hunger sensation or boost the feeling of fullness. However, so far there is no published evidence that I know of proving this new kind of aromatherapy can actually help weight loss. On-going studies do appear to show, however, that this approach to weight loss may in fact be highly effective in some individuals.

products available

Product	Manufacturer	Description
AromaScent Food Quenchers	Diet Pens Aromacology Corporation	Slimscents Small matchbox-size boxes impregnated with pure essential oils of bergamot, fennel and grapefruit

chewing gum
what is it?

The Geneva Diet offers a way of chewing yourself slim. The pack supplies a 15-day supply of sugar-free gum that contains 18 mcg of chromium picolinate per pellet. Four gums per day should be chewed at regular intervals between meals.

what is it supposed to do?

The chromium picolinate is supposed to help maintain steady blood sugar levels, helping to reduce sugar cravings and helping people avoid the urge to suddenly binge. Some experts also say that the action of chewing gum helps to release serotonin in the brain, which in turn reduces the appetite. The xylitol in the gum does at least help to prevent tooth decay.

susan says

This is being sold on the basis that the chromium will help to control appetite. See comments on chromium supplements (page 197).

who should avoid them?

Pregnant or breast-feeding women or anyone with a medical condition.

slimming patches
what are they?

Patches such as SlimSteady Dermopatch are plasters that release extracts of the seaweed *Fucus vesiculosis* into your system.

what are they supposed to do?

The manufacturers tell us that they gently release iodine into the bloodstream, which helps to gently stimulate the metabolism so your body works harder, increases energy levels and tones your muscles.

susan says

Iodine is essential for the normal functioning of the gland that produces the thyroid hormones. These hormones help to regulate metabolic rate. In the UK iodine deficiency is virtually unheard of today and there is no evidence that increasing the amount of iodine in the body increases metabolic rate.

drugs to aid weight **loss**

As with supplements, drugs aim to achieve one or more of three things to help people lose weight. They may be designed to help reduce the food consumed, reduce the amount of calories that the body absorbs, or increase the rate at which the body burns calories.

Most of the old drugs were appetite supplement amphetamine-based versions and were popular in the 1960s. Today we have a new generation of medicines that work by regulating the appetite and help to reduce the amount of food you eat. Another type work by stopping enzymes from breaking down fats. These lipase-inhibitors block the absorption of fat.

No drugs work without some lifestyle changes. They need to be combined with some effort from the person taking them such as an increase in exercise and changes in the foods and drinks consumed. They are aids, not substitutes for a weight loss program.

A doctor should take a full medical history prior to prescribing any weight-loss drug. If any relatives have or have had heart disease or diabetes or if you are or are trying to get pregnant or are breast-feeding, the chances are drugs are not for you. Doctors also tend not to prescribe drugs for weight loss unless you are of a weight that makes you obese, not simply overweight.

People with a history of an eating disorder, drug or alcohol abuse or those who are taking antidepressant medication are also not suitable candidates for these prescription medicines. Those with high blood pressure and glaucoma are usually also excluded.

appetite suppressants

Drugs that are designed to reduce hunger are called 'anorectic' agents. They work by affecting transmitters in the brain to reduce the perception of hunger.

amphetamines

The most widely used drugs in the 1960s and 1970s and a favourite with models of the time were the amphetamines. They were first made way back in the 1920s and were used as anticongestant inhalants before quickly being spotted as being good for diet-pills. Also called speed, pep pills or uppers, they are taken orally. Their effect is to decrease the appetite but at the same time have the unfortunate side-effect of also increasing heart rate and blood pressure. They increase the rate of breathing, lead to dizziness and aggressive behaviour.

People hooked on amphetamines for controlling their weight often end up feeling depressed, even though ironically they may have lost weight, as well as being very fatigued. Doctors tend not to prescribe them these days.

susan says

Amphetamines are potent drugs that should only be used under close medical supervision. They are extremely addictive. They are not appropriate at any time for the treatment of obesity since their side-effects greatly outweigh any modest effect on weight.

phentermine

An amphetamine-like drug that acts in the brain to suppress appetite.

susan says

Phentermine is not recommended for the treatment of obesity as it has a stimulant effect on the central nervous system and can be addictive.

fenfluramine/dexfenfluxamine

These two closely related drugs act to increase the concentration of serotonin in the brain, which then decreases appetite. People feel fuller more quickly and so eat less food.

susan says

In medically supervised clinical trails patients taking fenfluramine or dexfenfluramine lost significantly more weight than people taking a placebo. However, both drugs have now been withdrawn following reports that a small number of patients who had taken these drugs, including those using the phentermine/fenfluramine combination, were found to have heart valve defects.

'Fen-Phen'

The nickname given to fenfluramine/phentermine combinations which prior to withdrawal from the market had been available on prescription for about 25 years.

Discovered to be associated with some potentially rather dangerous side-effects involving increased risk of breathlessness, chest pain, faintness and swelling of the legs, it was also linked with primary pulmonary hypertension, a rare yet potentially fatal disorder that affects blood vessels in the lungs. These were the concerns leading to the removal of both drugs.

sibutramine

Available in the US as the drug called Meridia, this medicine works on the brain chemicals, helping to reduce appetite and give a sense of fullness. It seems to help people lose and keep weight off, with studies showing that people manage to burn off about 10% of their starting weight over a year. It is capable, however, of causing raised blood pressure and increasing the heart rate.

susan says

Sibutramine is currently available in Germany but

has not been given permission for use throughout Europe. It is therefore not available in the UK.

fat-blocking drugs

Since the appetite suppressants seem to come with the kind of side-effects most of us would prefer to avoid, it seems that the great hope of the diet industry currently lies with drugs that act as fat blockers.

orlistat

Sold as the drug Xenical, this drug quite literally interferes with the digestive enzymes that break down fat so it passes through the system undigested and appears as such at 'the other end'. Not to put too fine a point on it, this means that you get fatty stools. Up to 30% of the fat eaten can be lost in this way.

Xenical naturally has some drawbacks; not least that fat-soluble vitamins go flying out with the lost fat in the stools. That said, studies show that people who use this drug can lose about 10% of their initial weight over the course of a year.

susan says

Orlistat is the first of a new kind of treatment for obesity. It is now available throughout Europe, the US and in many other parts of the world. In the UK it is known as Xenical and is currently available on prescription for the medical treatment of obesity. Clinical trails of Orlistat have been conducted across the world and some patients have been treated contin-uously for two years with no adverse effects. Typical weight losses are about 10 kg in one year. About twice as many patients taking Orlistat lose 10% of their starting weight compared to those taking a placebo. Since Orlistat specifically targets dietary fat it can also help to reduce the level of fats in the blood. However, the downside is that it decreases the absorption of fat-soluble vitamins and some doctors recommend daily multivitamin supplement.

others
leptin

Produced naturally by fat cells, leptin acts on the brain to switch off hunger. Described as a 'magic' fat pill, leptin may help some overweight people regain control of excessive consumption but its mecha-nisms are still under investigation and there is no sign of it either becoming a cure-all or of being on prescription in the near future.

On future prescription drugs for obesity, Susan con-cludes:

A drug solution to weight problems does not look imminent. All the money being poured into obesity drug research is useful, however, because every week we find another part of the complicated jigsaw of appetite control. There is, though, a big lag between Sibutramine and Orlistat and the next drugs to make it to the overweight consumer.

food ingredients that help you slim
olestra

Not yet available in the UK, Olestra is a food ingredient used in products in the US that has the same 'feel' to the mouth and presence in foods as fat, but is not absorbed by the body. Scientists created Olestra by taking a normal fat molecule but changing its physical form so that normal fat-breaking enzymes in the digestive system can not break it down. This means that Olestra goes straight through the body and is not absorbed. If used to fry chips, Olestra reduces the calories by almost a third; when used to make a chocolate cake, some 70 calories are saved per serving. Vitamins A, D and E are believed to be lost from the body with Olestra, which worries some nutritionists. Of these, the loss of vitamin E is the biggest worry. New formulations of Olestra now have vitamin E added.

Olestra may help to lower the fat content of the diet, but it is not a quick-fix answer and does not mean you can freely indulge in foods containing it.

nutrasweet

An artificial, intense calorie-free sweetener used extensively in diet drinks and foods like yoghurts and fromage frais, Nutrasweet helps provide sweetness to the diet without the calories.

slimming machines and other gadgets

slendertone

Slendertone Body £99.95

Based on the concept of Electric Muscle Stimulation (EMS), the idea is that a Slendertone machine helps tone and work the muscles, contracting and relaxing them and helping you get results faster and more effectively than you can through exercise alone. Small pads are stuck to the body and supply impulses that make the muscle contract and relax 240 times in a 40-minute session.

Slendertone machines only work in conjunction with sensible eating and regular exercise.

phillips cellese cellulite massage system

£139.99

This is a 'vacumotion system' that gives an intense massage. The gadget has rollers and a suction chamber, which are said to reduce the fatty cells deep in the skin and presumably help reduce cellulite.

No published evidence appears to be yet available to prove that this product works.

gaia electrolipolysis machine

£35 per session

Hailed as the completely new way to remove unwanted fat without effort or discomfort, many people are said to 'shrink' by at least one whole size after the first treatment. Electrical currents are transmitted to the fat cells via self-adhesive electrodes stuck to the skin. The stimulation apparently goes on inside the actual fat cells where triglycerides are changed to free fatty acids so that they can be excreted in tissue fluid. From here they are transported into the lymph system. The lymph drainage system is then stimulated, which helps 'get rid of' the fatty acids, which are excreted in the urine.

On-going trials.

Whichever, if any, of these products you think could be worth using in your 15-day program please remember, they can only be an adjunct to the rest of the advice in this book never a replacement.

So what are you waiting for? Let's get going – you sexy thing.

index

A-line skirts 171
abdomen 179
  compression 135
  curls 127
  exercise 130
Achilles tendon 171
adrenaline 160
advertising 15
aerobic exercise 119, 120
  see also calorie-burning
    work
aftershave 201
age 117
alcohol 190
allergies 202
alternate arm/leg raises 125
Amazon 159, 217
amino acids 209, 211, 213
aminophylline 196
amphetamines 215, 231, 232
anaemia 207
ankles 171, 198
antioxidants 183
antiperspirants 201
aphrodisiacs 148–61

Aphrodite 148
appearance 163–4
apple pectin 224
Arabs 157
Aristotle 1
arms 165
Aromacology Corporation
  229
AromaScent Diet Pens 228
aromatherapy 194–5, 198,
  228
artichokes 197–8, 200
ASDA 70, 72
Asia 157, 160
asparagus 150
astralagus 161
atherosclerosis 111–12
avocado pears 153

back exercise 132
bacon dishes
  bacon and egg crumpets
    63–4
  bacon, lettuce and tomato
    (BLT) sandwich 68–9

bacon sandwich 37
bad breath 202
baked potatoes 27–8, 45
baked sweet potato with
    crunchy bacon topping
    78–80
balance 111
bananas 151–2
barley bran 224
basic metabolic rate (BMR)
    114–16
beaches 165–6
beans on toast 38
beer bellies 178
belts 174, 175, 178
bikinis 165, 166
bile 225
blood chemistry 14
blood pressure 111–12, 161,
    214–15, 217, 232
blood sugar 22, 26, 156, 197,
    222, 229
blouson jackets 178
body alignment 181
Body Breakthrough 218
Bond, J 6
bones 106–7, 111, 117
Boots 40–1, 44–5
borax 157–8
bottom 165–6, 173–5, 179,
    181, 184
Bowskill, J 12
box pleats 173

boxer shorts 169
braces 178
braiding 173
brain chemistry 14
bran and fruit quick start 32
bras 167, 173, 176
Brazil 159
breakfasts 29, 31, 32–8
breastfeeding 207, 209–10,
    230–31
Briffa, J 192
broccoli and almond soup
    64–5
broken veins 183–4
bronzing powder 176
builder's bottom 178
bulgar wheat pilaff with
    apricots 90–1
burgers 27
Burke, K 190, 193
bust 165–6, 173, 176–7
buttocks 181
buttons 177

caffeine 156, 188, 190, 196,
    214–17
calorie-burning work 138–46
    see also aerobic exercise
calves 171
Calvin Klein 169
cami-knickers 167
capsicum 219
carbohydrates 20, 21–6, 31

metabolism 211
products 208, 220
carrots 161
cashew nut rice salad with
    mango 50–1
cat lift 136–7
cedar 195
cellulite 185–200, 238
centella asiatica 195–6, 197
champagne 156
changes 1–2, 9–10, 231
Cheat at Slimming 163
chemistry 14–28
chemists 201
cherries 153
chest 179
  exercise 129
chestnuts 195
chewing gum 200, 229–30
chicken dishes:
  chicken Caesar salad 61–2
  chicken noodle soup 53–4
  chicken salad with
    horseradish dressing
    82–3
  chicken teriyaki 77–8
  fried chicken 27
chickpea casserole with
    cous cous 75–7
chickpea soup with mint
    59–61
chickweed 200
chillies 157, 211

China 158, 160, 161
Chinese take-aways 27
chitosan 225–6
chocolate 149, 155–6
cholesterol 112, 220, 225
chromium 205–6, 208, 229
Chrysler, W 12
chrysocalla 157–8
Churchill, W 12
cigar pants 174
cinnamon 155
citrus fibre concentrate 224
Clarins 183
cleavage 176
clinical trials 197, 235
clinics 203
clothes 163, 170–9
cluster beans 222
coconuts 162
cod with lime and coriander
    dressing 100–1
Cohen, P 1–5, 7–12
collars 176
colours 165–6, 168–9, 174–5,
    177
conditioning exercises
    121–2, 138–47, 181
confidence 163–4, 198
constipation 188, 202
control panels 167–8
control-top tights 169
cooking 26
cool-down exercises 119–20

coriander 154–5
corn bran 224
cornflakes 35–6
cottage pie 98–9
cotton 169
counselling 2
crab-stuffed coriander pittas 47–8
crash diets 202
cravings 11, 19, 21–2, 229
creams 195–6, 198
creatine 212–13
croissants 32
Crown, S 156
cruise-cut trousers 172
cup sizes 176
curried chickpea soup with mint 59–61
cypress 195

Daily Express 163
Daily Mail 163
dancing 118
Dancy, E. 185, 196
Danone Actimel 35
dehydration 11, 202
delectable dinners 75–101
dental hygienists 200
dentists 201, 202
deodorants 201
Descartes, R 12
desires 2–4, 8, 10, 12, 17
dexfenfluramine 233

diabetes 206, 231
digestive system 202, 220–21, 234
dinners 29, 31, 70–101
dips 124
doctors 119, 161, 199, 202, 221, 231–2
dong quai 160
door pull-ups 125
double-breasted suits 177
dresses 170–5
drugs 231–9

egg and mushrooms 38
eggs 148
Einstein, A 12
elasticated waists 178
elbows 183
Electric Muscle Stimulation (EMS) 238
Encyclopaedia Britannica 148
endocrine glands 160
endorphins 111, 156
England 158
enzymes 110, 196, 200, 209, 231, 234, 237
ephedra 215
ephedrine 214, 215
escalators 118
essential fatty acids (EFAs) 20–1, 26, 31
essential oils 194–5

Estée Lauder 183
eucalyptus 195
Europe 235, 236
evolution 15, 108
exercises 12, 30
  cellulite 186, 191–4
  15-day plan 106–47
  desire 3–4
  posture 180–1
  products 212, 216, 231
exfoliation 182–3
expectations 7–10, 13

fabrics 175
fake tan 169, 182–4
fantasies 150–3
fast food 26–8
fat 17–22, 26, 31
  blockers 225–7, 231, 234–6
  men 177–8
Fat Magnets 227
Fen-Phen 234
fenfluramine 233–4
fennel 46–7
fibre 220–22, 224
fibroblasts 196
figs 152
fishnets 169
fit fix 33
flannel 175
flavonoids 197
flexibility 128
flossing 200

food allergies 202
food ingredients 237
free radicals 196
French toast 36
fried chicken 27
fruit compote on rye 34
fruit salad 33
fruits 202, 220

G-strings 167
gabardine 175
gadgets 238–9
Gaia Electrolipolysis
    machine 238–9
galanin 19
game 17
Gap 169
Garcinia cambogia 207, 209
gardening 118
garlic 158–9
gathered skirts 173
gels 195–6
Geneva Diet 229
Germany 236
GI, see glycaemic index
ginger 219
gingivitis 202
ginkgo biloba 159–60, 197
ginseng 149, 153, 160–1
girdle of strength 181
glucomannan 221
glycaemic index (GI)
    numbers 23–5

goals 4, 8, 10, 164
grab and go breakfasts 35–6
grace 111
grapes 153, 197
grilled paprika salmon with
    potato-and-grain mustard
    salad 55–6
grilled pork escalopes with
    parsley and mustard
    mash 86–8
grooming kits 201
guar gum 222
guarana 217
gums 200, 202

hairdressers 164
halitosis 202
hamstrings 128
Hard Rock Café 71
hazelnut oil 196
HCA, *see* hydroxycitrate
hearty minestrone with
    bacon 96–7
hedera helix 195
Hello! 163
hemlines 170–2
Hepburn, A 156
Herbal v-X 159
Herbal v-Y 159
herbalists 158, 222
herpes simplex 211
hiatus hernia 202
high GI foods 24–5

high heels 164, 172, 175
hip flexors 128–9
Hippocrates 152
hips 166, 171–2, 174–5
Holford, P 206, 208
Holland and Barratt 219,
    223, 224
home-made rolls 40
home-made sandwiches 39
home-toning machines
    179–80
honey 152
honey, oat bran and barley
    bread 34
hormones 19–20, 22–3, 109,
    160, 205, 230
horsetail 198
hosiery 168, 171
hot croissants 32
housework 118
5-HTP, *see*
    5-hydroxytriptophan
Human Nutrition Research
    204
humous on toasted rye 49–50
hunger 15–25, 26, 30, 46
    reducing products 213,
    220–24
    smell 228
hunter-gatherers 15
Hurley, L 8
hydroxycitrate (HCA)
    207–209

5-hydroxytriptophan
(5-HTP) 213–14
hypothalamus 15–16, 213

ice cream 149, 156
imagination 4–6, 10, 13, 16
India 207
Indian take-aways 27
Institute of Biosexology,
    Paris 159
insulin 20, 22–3, 26, 205–6
intestines 222
inulin sugar beet fibre
    concentrate 224
iodine 197, 230
Ionothermie 199
ivy 195

jacket potatoes 27–8, 45
jackets 175–9
jeans 174
Jebb, S 204, 206–8, 210, 212
    products 220–21, 226, 228,
    233–6
    stimulants 214
jumpers 175–6, 178

kebab houses 27
kelp 197
kidney bean pulao 88–90
kidneys 207, 210
Kira 160
knees 171, 183

knickers 164, 167–8
knits 178
kola nut 219
konjac plant 221

L-arginine 211–12
L-carnitine 209–10
lampshade shape 171
Larkhill Green Farm 223,
    227
laxatives 223
Le Roc 183
legs 172, 184–200
leisurely breakfast treats
    36–8
lemon 195
length of skirts 170–2
leptin 236
Lichtwer Pharma 198
lifestyle 231
lipase-inhibitors 231
liver 207
Love Bites 29, 31, 39, 101–5
    see also snacks
low GI foods 23–4
lower abdominal
    compression 135
lunches 29, 31, 39–69
lunges 124
lycra 168
lymph drainage system 185,
    188, 191, 192, 195,
    198–200, 239

lysine 209

Ma huang 215
mackerel and mango salad
    85–6
magazines 163, 203
make-up 176
Manchuria 160
mangos 156
manicures 201
manual lymphatic drainage
    199
manufacturers 204, 218–9,
    221, 230
Marie Antoinette, Queen 156
Marks and Spencers 169
masseurs 199
meals 26–8, 30
    see also breakfasts;
        dinners; lunches
meat 17
Medical Research Council
    204
medium GI foods 24–5
Melrose Place 183
men 116–17, 154, 157
    aphrodisiacs 159–61
    fat 177–8
    nails 201
    short 177
    swimwear 166
    tall 177
    underwear 167, 169

menopause 160
Menzies, J. 163–4, 168, 170,
    172–4, 176, 179–82
Meridia 235
mesotherapy 191
metabolism 30, 107–9,
    113–18, 121
    carbohydrates 211
    products 204–6, 209
    stimulants 214–19
methionine 209
methyl xanthins 215, 217
methylcellulose 224
microcirculation 183, 195,
    198
micronutrients 207
mind power 1–13
minerals 31, 151, 159, 200,
    205–6
minestrone with bacon 96–7
mini-skirts 171
mitts 183
moisturizing tights 169
Moroccan chickpea
    casserole with couscous
    75–7
mouth washes 200
movies 164
muffin pizzas with quorn
    and tomato 56–8
muira puama 159
Murray, M 208
muscles 106–10, 116–18, 121

posture 179, 181
products 206, 209, 211, 216
skeletal 212
slimming machines 238
mushrooms 154, 225
mustard seeds 219

nails 201
Naseem, P 7
neck lift 134
necklines 177
negative thinking 4, 7–9
newspapers 163, 203
nicotine 214
no-cook meals 26
Nutrasweet 237–8
nylon 169

obliques 123
oesophagus 223
Olestra 237
optical illusions 164, 165–79, 170
Orlistat 234–5, 236
overweight people 5, 11, 107, 208, 236
oysters 148, 151, 159

padded bras 176
pampering 163
pants 169
parsnips 161

Passion International 218–19
pasta salad with prawns and lemon dressing 58–9
patterns 165, 177
Pavarotti, L 178
pear-shaped women 165–6, 170
pedicures 201
pendants 176–7
penguin extension 136
penne pasta salad with prawns and lemon dressing 58–9
pepper-crusted cod with lime and coriander dressing 100–1
perfume 201
peroxide 164
personal hygiene 201
Peter Black Healthcare 224
phentermine 233, 234
phenylethylamine 156
pheromones 201
Phillips Cellese Cellulite Massage System 238
Pilates, J 181
pinstripes 177
plantains 222
plaque 200
pleats 177, 178
Pompadour, Mme de 154
pools 165–6, 184

pork escalopes with parsley and mustard mash 86–8
positive thinking 3–4
posture 132–3, 138, 140–1
  exercises 143–6, 179–81
  tips 163–4
potatoes 27–8, 45
poultry 17
Powers, A 6
pregnancy 195, 207, 209–11, 230–231
prescription drugs 161, 231–6
Pretty Polly 169
probiotics 220
product assessments 203–39
professional treatments 199
protein 16–21, 26, 30, 211, 213
psyllium husks 222–3
Ptychopetalum olacoides 159
push-ups 123

quadriceps flexors 128–9
quick meals
  breakfasts 32–6
  dinners 70–5
  lunches 39–45
raspberry muffins 33–4
rating of perceived exertion (RPE) 120–1
re-training 19
ready-meals 70–5

recipes 29–105
red kidney bean pulao 88–90
red peppers 148
repetition 6, 10, 121
resistance exercises 121–2, 206
reverse curls 126
rhino horn 149, 162
ribs 179, 181
rice cakes 44
rice and fish cakes 92–3
rice noodle stir-fry with shitake mushrooms 94–5
Roberts, J 184
Robinson, L 181
rolls 40
Rumbler's Cornflakes 35–6

Safeway 42, 74–5
sage 195
Sainsbury's 42
St John's wort 160
St Michael 41, 43, 70, 72, 74
St Tropez Fake Tan 183
salad niçoise with grilled tuna 52–3
salmon dishes
  salmon and fennel crispbreads 46–7
  salmon with potato-and-grain mustard salad 55–6
  salmon with sautéed sprouting beans 80–1

salon treatments 184
sandals 168
sandwiches 31, 39, 39–43,
    68–9
saponins 160
sardines on toast 66–7
scarves 176
Schiff 218
Schwartzenegger, A 109
sclerotherapy 184
seaweed 197
serotonin 213, 229, 233
sex 111–12, 148–50
shellfish 225, 226
shirt-style dresses 174
shirts 176, 177, 178
shop lunches 43–5
shop sandwiches 40–3
shopping lists 10
short men 177
shoulders 179, 181
    exercise 131
    padding 173
    squeeze 133–4
Sibutramine 235–6
side-effects 214, 232–3
silica 200
silicum 196, 198
single-breasted suits 177
skin 163, 164, 182–200
skin brushing 198
skirts 170–5
sleep 112–13

Slendertone 238
slimming
    food ingredients 237
    machines 238–9
    patches 230
Slimscents 229
smell 154–5, 228
smoked haddock omelette
    37
snacks 26–8, 29
soups 44, 59–61, 96–7
South America 217
soya fibre 224
Spanish fly 162
Spice Girls 2, 4
spicy bulgar wheat pilaff
    with apricots 90–1
spicy rice and fish cakes
    92–3
spine 181
Spitz, M 166
spots 165
squats 122
stained teeth 200
stairs 118
stallion genitalia 158
Stallone, S 109
steamed salmon with
    sautéed sprouting beans
    80–1
step-ups 126
sternum 179
stilettos 164

stimulants 214–19
stockings 168
stomach 165, 169, 178–9, 181, 202, 222–3
straps 165
strawberries 154
strengthening exercises 107–10, 117, 121–2, 138–47
stress 112, 118, 217
stretching 128, 139, 141, 143–4
stripes 165, 173
sugar 22, 190
suits 177–8
supplements 196–8, 231
survival mechanisms 18, 108
sushi 44
sweaters 173–4
sweet potatoes 78–80
swimming costumes 165–6
Swiss Health 218

T-shirts 178
tall men 177
tamarinds 207
tannins 197
tans 182–3
taste 155–6
teeth 200, 202, 229
television 164
Tesco 43, 70, 73
testosterone 160, 161

thighs 165, 170–3, 174, 184
thiomucase 196, 200
Thompson Medical Company 224
thongs 167
thorn apples 157
throat 222, 223
thyroid 230
Tiberius, Emperor 162
ties 179
tights 168–9, 175
time 9–14
tofu and noodle soup 83–4
toothpastes 200
training 107–9, 117, 120–1, 206
  see also exercises
trapezius exercise 130
treatments 184, 201
triceps exercise 131
triglycerides 239
trousers 172–4, 178
truffles 154
trunks 166
tryptophan 213
tulip-shaped skirts 171, 173
tummy, see stomach
tunic tops 174
turn-ups 177

underwear 167–8
United Kingdom (UK) 215, 235–7

United States (US) 215, 235, 237

V-neck jumpers 176
V-shaped bodices 172
Vaughan, P 26, 31
vegetables 31, 202, 220
Viagra 158
visible panty line (VPL) 164, 167
vitamins 31, 235, 237
vitis vinifera 197

waistbands 178, 179
waistcoats 178
waistline 173, 175
Waitrose 41, 71
walking 118, 120
warm-up exercises 119, 120
water 11
Weight Watchers 73

weight-loss products 203–238
white thorn apples 157
will-power 14
winter 18
wired bras 176
withdrawal periods 19
women 116–17, 154, 157
    aphrodisiacs 159–61
    nails 201
    swimwear 165–6
    underwear 167
wrap-around skirts 173, 175

X-Fat UK 227
Xenical 234–5
xylitol 200, 229

yoghurt and fruit mix 35
yohimbe 161

Thorsons

Be inspired to change your life